INLAND CRUISING
A Guide to Boating on Canals and Rivers

INLAND CRUISING

A Guide to Boating on Canals and Rivers

Norman Alborough

The Crowood Press

First published in 1995 by
The Crowood Press Ltd
Ramsbury, Marlborough
Wiltshire SN8 2HR

© Norman Alborough 1995

British Library Cataloguing-in-Publication Data
A catalogue record for this book is available from the British
Library.

ISBN 1 85223 876 3

Dedication
To my wife Linda for all her love and support.

Picture Credits
All photographs are by Norman Alborough, except those on pages 19, 21, 22, 23, 24,
and 26, which are by Graham Fisher, and those on pages 37 and 39 (bottom),
which are by Mel Booth.
All line drawings are by Claire Upsdale-Jones, except those on pages
22, 23, 84, 117 (bottom) and 118 (bottom), which are by Bob Constant.

Printed and bound in Great Britain by The Bath Press

Contents

Acknowledgements

There are a large number of people who have helped me with the compilation of this book and whom I would like to thank, principally, Nick Billingham, my friend and Technical Editor of *Canal & Riverboat*, and Graham Fisher who submitted a number of photographs, which are credited within the text.

I am also grateful to the following for their assistance in one form or another: Harry Arnold of Waterway Images; British Waterways and Limehouse Marina; Lee Valley Regional Park Authority and in particular Paul Richardson; Willowtree Marina and in particular Arthur Bennett and Beth Walker; Jack and Sheila Graham and all the team at South Shore Narrowboats based at Aynho Wharf; Peter Topping and his Cowroast Team at Fenny Compton Marina; Linda Millward at Teddesley Boat Company; Alasdair and Hannah Lawrance at Swallow Cruisers; and not least the members of the St Pancras Cruising Club.

Also a big thank you goes out to all the unknown inland waterways boaters who happened to be 'in shot' when I was out and about with my camera.

Finally, my thanks go to Terence Morgan, publisher of *Canal & Riverboat*, without whom I would not have been in the position of editing the magazine in the first place, and also to Bill Sherry who has always given his dedication and support.

Preface

When I was approached with a view to writing a book about boat handling on inland waterways I realized that I would have the opportunity of interpreting the knowledge I had accumulated over the years at *Canal & Riverboat* in a coherent form. As editor I have seen and read of so many people's boat-handling experiences that I have found common factors which could usefully be passed on to others. In writing this book there was a standard to be achieved; it was a task to be undertaken with pride.

I have therefore compiled a book in which you get advice, sensible advice, when you need it; a book to be there as a companion and a friend, not dictating or pointing an accusatory finger. No book could ever aspire to be the be-all and end-all of a subject. There will always be something different, something which is completely individualistic about any book, as books emerge out of a combination of circumstances. However, in this book I have attempted to include all the most frequently encountered situations.

The subject falls naturally into two distinct categories: canal cruising and river cruising. Your past and current experience, however much you have, will depend very much on the types of boat you have taken out on the water. Again, much will also depend on the amount of responsibility you have had or now enjoy.

As with all instructional publications such as this there are bound to be some grey areas. There may be some aspects you have avoided out of choice or perhaps never had the opportunity to encounter. Some forms of boating are unique to a particular area and so are only to be met with occasionally. When tackling the inland waterways, it is a full appreciation of the complete boating experience that gives you confidence. Combine this with talking to other boaters and you can begin to form a picture of what inland boating is all about.

Obviously, the more often you have the chance to get afloat, the steeper your individual learning curve will be compared to that of the occasional boater. The challenge that lies around every bend is part of the joy of canals. Your ability to cope will be reflected in what you are capable of achieving. This book should give you some idea of what to expect and how to deal with certain situations if they arise.

I wonder how your personal ideals and methods concerning boat handling compare with other people's? Boating is fun and always should be and your knowledge of the subject should make it so. A lack of this may tarnish your viewpoint. I very much hope this book will help.

— 1 —
Planning the Cruise

A Voyage of Discovery

An island race ... the sea in one's blood ... maritime folk ... these are just a few of the old clichés spouted over the years about the British and the unbreakable link between the sea and our island. Far more importantly, however, in the British Isles we do not have to rely on the sea for our boating and marine pleasures. We have our own unique inland waterways system. A combination of man-made canals and river navigations, many of which were created over 200 years ago, allow the British access to untold wonders of boating. This offers a completely different perspective to maritime life and yet provides the opportunity to undertake your own voyage of discovery.

With over 2,000 miles of navigable waterways from which to choose, ranging from North Yorkshire to the South of England, from North Wales to East Anglia, the variety of cruising area is quite incredible. Such a plethora of canals and rivers might initially appear daunting. Where do you begin? There are many guidebooks to help you make your decision but in the end where you go will depend very much on the type of boating you want to try and the type of boat being made available to you.

That decision is entirely up to you but will relate to your ability and experience, and the availability of boat, of course. Your knowledge of inland waterways will normally be a combination of the theoret-

ical with the practical; both aspects are equally important. Somebody who reads every publication, article or feature may feel that they are completely *au fait* with all possibilities; it is only when the practicalities are forced upon the boater that applying the theory may turn out to be not quite so easy.

If you are new to the inland scene you are going to want to take things steadily. Obviously this will mean selecting a cruising area that is pretty straightforward. Only when you've mastered that is it time to progress. Wherever you choose to go, and whatever the type of boat, it's going to be an exciting experience.

Where to Cruise?

A careful study of a map of the inland waterways of the British Isles shows definite concentrations of canal and river navigations in the Midlands and the north-west, and running down in a south-easterly direction towards the London area. The waterway links, some of which were built 200 years ago or more, were designed to connect the main centres of industry as they existed in the late eighteenth and early nineteenth centuries. The Rivers Trent, Thames, Severn and Mersey were, as they still are, the principal rivers of the country and the canals were constructed between them to ensure there was an easier flow of goods across areas of land where there was no

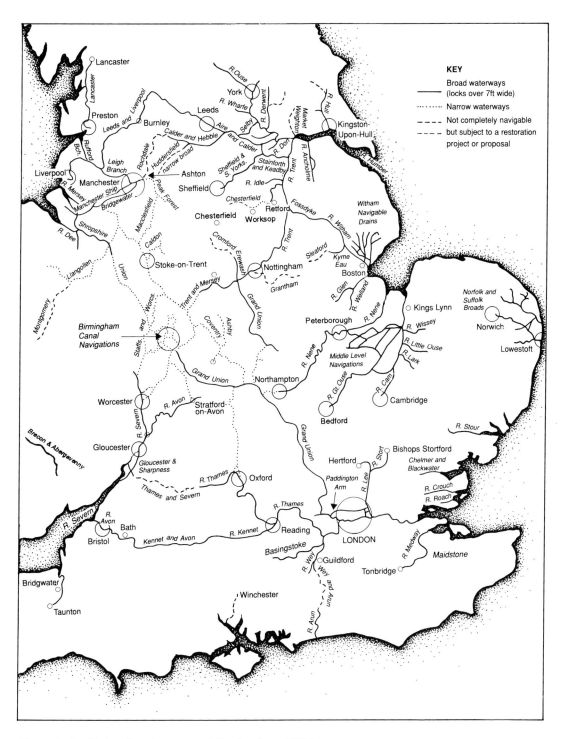

The principal inland waterways of England and Wales.

The choice is yours! Any direction, it's entirely up to you. Signposts such as this really do put canal boating in perspective.

navigable river. The principle behind the 'Grand Cross' idea of connecting the rivers with a canal system can be read about in greater depth in many books describing the history of the inland waterways system of the British Isles.

Of course the first-time boater is not encouraged to use only the canal system. The River Thames, flowing east from Gloucestershire to London, is one of the most popular and beautiful waterways in this country and can provide some wonderful cruising. Like all rivers, it flows downhill towards the sea, so there are a number of locks situated at fairly regular

intervals along its length. On the Thames these are all manned by lock keepers employed by the National Rivers Authority (NRA) whose job it is to ensure the smooth passage of boats and boaters along the river. It is all very straightforward and part of the enjoyment of cruising this magnificent river. Following a guidebook or map of the river is a fascinating process as you pass so many places of interest on your journey. Planning ahead where to moor either at lunchtimes or at the end of the cruising day is equally exciting. It is important to discuss such matters with the crew so it is a jointly reached decision. Total involvement is the name of the game when it comes to inland waterways boating and a contribution from each and every one is necessary if the whole cruise is going to be an outstanding success.

You will see on the map of the waterways system a considerable number of navigations in the east of England, particularly through Cambridgeshire, which are known as the Middle Level Navigations, and further east in East Anglia itself where the Broads straddle the counties of Norfolk and Suffolk. The Norfolk Broads are probably the most popular cruising area in this country and it is here, on the waters of the Rivers Bure, Yare, Waveney, Thurne and Ant, that vast numbers of boaters cut their boating teeth. The initial experience of cruising on the Norfolk Broads is one that is never forgotten and if you become hooked on the area you will return time and time again.

There are two types of canal on the canal system which are differentiated on the map – namely, broad canals and narrow canals. In most cases the broad canals were built first in the construction of the system and it was possible for boats not only to pass each other easily in either direction on the pounds (the length of

Canal bridges – many old and showing signs of wear – are part of a waterway's history and character.

waterway between each lock), but also to moor abreast in the broad locks themselves. When canals were first being built there was a lot of money available from the individual canal companies and many of these made sure that it was possible to transport goods and then more goods as lively competition between them stimulated growth.

Later, as the Canal Age, as it became known, progressed, money to fund canal construction was not so freely available. Competition naturally remained but the beginning of the Railway Age was taking the gloss off the initial boom. Therefore to save money, whilst still reaching the planned destination, it was decided to build narrow canals. These were basically

half the width of their broad predecessors, and although it was still possible for the narrow-beam boats to pass each other on the pounds the narrow locks prohibited this and only one boat was allowed to pass through the lock itself, either up or down, at any time.

The narrow canals can be seen as the veins of the inland waterways system, and the broad canals as the arteries. If you are planning a canal boating cruise you can experience both types. Broad and narrow canals require different boat-handling knowledge, but just look at the map again. Look at the towns and main centres. A larger-scale map will show you which villages are located en route. Make your judgement, if it's your first time on the

A holiday hire fleet at its moorings, all waiting for the off!

canal system or on a river, by taking all these factors into account. You may choose to go boating in an area you know well but you will be surprised, I can assure you, when you are out on the water passing through a town as opposed to travelling through by car. It is completely different. You will see and appreciate a totally new side of a community from a waterway. You will come across places you would not have believed existed, and indeed a whole new way of life.

The final decision on selecting a cruising area will depend on many factors. What is certain is that once you have made up your mind you won't regret it wherever you go. After all, with such a tremendous selection available there will always be another time to explore somewhere else.

Hiring for Your Holiday

There are now so many companies involved in hiring out narrow boats and cruisers on our inland waterways system that, on the face of it, it seems quite a difficult task to decide which company to choose. If you are intending to cruise our canals and rivers and you don't own your own boat then the hire companies have a great deal to offer the prospective holiday-maker.

So to start with, how do you decide which company to choose, which company has the best boats or is in the area where you would like to spend your precious week or fortnight? Which company can provide the holiday you are looking for? Do you want to have a boat that is basically a home from home, providing every facility? How much are you expecting to pay? How much are you prepared to pay? All these factors have to be taken into consideration, as well as discussing them with the family/friends who are to accompany you, before deciding where you want to go.

So you pick an area that perhaps you have not cruised before, or a canal or river that you liked so much the first time that you wish to experience its delights again. Now is the time for looking at advertisements and guides, and contacting the companies concerned to ask for their individual brochures. The quality of such brochures varies from company to company but they are all, of course, endeavouring to provide as good a service as each other for the boater. When you receive the brochure from the boatyard have a good look at it and check up on all the different points you feel to be important when boating.

Looking at the Brochures

If you find a particular boat in the brochure appealing, look carefully at its layout and interior plan and check that it comes up to your expectations. It might even be worth while for those boaters who live not too far away from the boatyard to pay a visit to see for themselves both what the yard and the boats are like.

The photographs of narrow boats and motor cruisers that appear in the

Guidebooks, maps and cruising information – all there to help you on your way. They are available at most chandleries and marinas.

brochures are obviously taken at the best possible time when the boats are probably new and the weather conditions are ideal. So it could be that when you arrive for your boating holiday the boat of your choice might not be quite as smart as first appearances indicated. The numerous holiday boat-hiring companies vary in size from having only one or two boats in the fleet to having over sixty or seventy, but having large numbers in a fleet doesn't necessarily mean that the boats are all of excellent quality. You can often experience boating holidays with very small companies who provide a marvellous service, whereas on occasion the boats in a larger company leave something to be desired. Small firms often pride themselves on the fact that they can offer excellent service – but it's impossible to make generalizations and at the end of the day it's really all a question of careful selection.

Think carefully about who is going to go on the holiday with you and the needs of particular individuals. These may include elderly grandparents or young children. Make sure you select a boat that will be easy enough to move about in safely, and one that should be fairly straightforward to handle. If you already have experience of inland waterways boating you will know to a greater or lesser extent what to expect. If the area you choose for boating has many locks then obviously your holiday will be pretty active and not quite so relaxed, but then again full of fun. Older people may not necessarily want to get

A range of inland cruisers – all shapes and varieties. Here, hard-standing craft give potential boat buyers an opportunity for all-round inspection.

involved in lock working whilst younger boaters will certainly enjoy the rigours of the experience.

If you don't want to experience locks at all then it is suggested that you try the companies based on lock-free canals or go river cruising. The River Thames and Norfolk Broads both have a tremendous amount to offer and it is on such rivers that many boaters first get bitten by the boating bug. There are a great number of companies based on these waterways who provide somewhat different services to those offered by narrow boat companies, but then again the environment on the Broads and the Thames is very different from that on smaller canals.

An important aspect to bear in mind when selecting a boat is the number of people to be catered for. You should look at a boat with slightly more berths than the number actually needed. As an example, a family of four could find it somewhat cramped on a four-berth boat, while on a six-berth boat there would be ample space for just spreading out. Similarly, a party of six or two families of four making up eight would probably have more room on a ten- or twelve-berth boat. This all depends on how friendly everyone is with one another and on occasion, of course, lack of space is not regarded as a problem.

Prices and Facilities

A great deal will depend on how much the actual boat costs for one week or two, and it's really a good idea to divide the cost of a week's holiday between the number of people going. This puts the amount being charged more in perspective. The price is variable, depending on the time of year you want to go boating. Early and late season, which could be anything from mid-April to mid-May, or late September to late October, will generally be cheaper; high season, which basically means June, July and August, will be more expensive. Check the brochure carefully on prices and remember also to note whether they include VAT. Look out as well for the little extras that may or may not be included. The small print could say, for example, that the price does not include bed linen or a television and it's worth checking if this is indeed the case or not.

Many boaters are prepared for somewhat basic facilities as this is how they feel canal boating should be. This can mean that a Porta Potti would be included rather than a flush toilet with holding tank. All this information can be gleaned from the brochure and if you have any other queries you feel need answering then the boatyard should be only too happy to explain further. There are a large number of superb boats now available for holiday hiring, both motor cruisers and narrow boats, so every taste can be catered for.

If you are taking younger children along on your cruise make sure as well that there are facilities such as buoyancy aids, and bear in mind that if you are choosing a traditional style of narrow boat then there won't be the room on the stern for families. Compare this, however, with the cruiser style of narrow boat, where there *is* room.

There's another option now open to you: short break offers are at present being made increasingly popular by hiring companies. If you just want a weekend getaway on the canals or a mid-week break you'll find some very good bargain offers available. If you are a complete novice to the world of inland waterways boating such a taster could be just the thing you are looking for. Once you've tried it, it can practically be guaranteed that you'll want to do it again and probably for a longer spell afloat!

Planning the Itinerary

When you have eventually decided on which boat you are going to spend your holiday, and which company will have the pleasure of providing it, then it's time to start planning your cruise. Buy the guidebooks and read the articles in *Canal & Riverboat* and *Waterways World* about those canals you hope to visit. From them you should be able to get plenty of ideas on where it would be worth while mooring for the night and so on.

Good luck with your holiday narrow boat or motor cruiser hiring and let's hope that the boats you select are exactly as you would wish them to be. It is certain that you will enjoy boating on inland waterways and find it an experience to savour and repeat time and time again. Moreover the hiring companies are sure to feel likewise!

— 2 —

Choosing the Boat for You

A walk along a canalside towpath or the embankment of a river will soon make it very apparent what a range of craft there is to be seen on our inland waterways. Very often boats seem to be out of place and do not relate to any style or form in particular. However, it will soon become quite obvious that there are a number of restrictions that apply to boating on canals and rivers and that therefore the boats that use them have been designed accordingly.

As mentioned in the previous chapter, for the most part canals are narrow while rivers are frequently very wide indeed. The general terminology of 'narrow boats' and 'inland motor cruisers' really divides the steel-constructed craft from those made of glass-reinforced plastic (GRP). The type of boat that you, the boater, will want will depend on where you have decided to go cruising. Narrow-beam boats are naturally more suitable for use on canals whilst broad-beam ones are designed for use on rivers and wider open spaces.

When the canals were first built the boats that used them had to be narrow – 6ft 10in beam. It had to be possible for such craft to pass one another and at the same time utilize the space within its length efficiently. Therefore the optimum shape of the narrow boat, or barge if it was for carrying goods, was for the overall length to be limited to the maximum

A most novel variation on the theme of trailability. This particular vessel can be used in either boat or caravan mode.

length of locks to be negotiated on the route. As the canal system expanded these specifications tended to vary but on the whole there was a form of standardization which those folk who built the boats had to adhere to if they were going to be of any use at all.

Nowadays, naturally, the division is clear between steel narrow boats and fibreglass cruisers and if you are contemplating boating on either canals or rivers you will have to make your mind up as to which type you want to choose. They each have their own advantages and disadvantages; it's just a question of style, matching the boat you are on to the type of person you are. Whatever best meets your requirements will obviously be the boat for you.

However, it's not quite as easy as that! If you look carefully, whilst gazing from the towpath, you will certainly note a number of variations on the theme. You need to be aware of the choice of style available as subtle differences in appearance can affect not only the structure and composition but also how the interior is fitted out. It can be somewhat confusing on occasion. Terminology used by boat builders categorizes narrow boats as cruiser style, traditional style, Joshers, tugs and semi-traditional style; their different shapes within the general overall appearance of the narrow boat once again bring advantages and disadvantages.

Styles of Narrow Boat

The Cruiser Style

The cruiser style is probably the most commonly seen narrow boat on the inland waterways today. The shape reflects the old Grand Union Star working boat and in many ways its structure combines with a

river boat. On such boats the obvious features are the large stern and front decks, which, although they take up a fair amount of the overall length available, allow members of the crew to stay outside the confines of the boat's interior and appreciate the scenery as the cruise progresses. Such boats are popular with families as this deck space, when translated into holiday enjoyment, offers the opportunity to chat with others, soak up the sun, have a drink, eat a meal – all as the boat passes silently over the water. You will therefore appreciate that when it

The view from the rear deck of a traditional narrow boat looking through the boatman's cabin towards the engine room beyond. Note also the traditional form of steering with wheel and gear lever.

A cruiser-style narrow boat with spacious rear deck and room for crew. This is an Anglo-Welsh hire boat.

A selection of narrow boats showing a few of the myriad different styles, shapes and sizes possible. The combinations are endless and no two boats are exactly the same.

comes to hire-boating holidays and boats available, the cruiser style far out-numbers other forms of narrow boat.

The Traditional Style

What is known as the traditional style (or 'trad') is very much derived from the old style of working boat and how that style accommodated the working boatman and his cargo. On today's traditional narrow boat the cargo is more often than not the crew, who utilize the space for day-to-day living. Towards the rear of the boat the boatman's cabin and engine room have been retained and this means that the stern deck is small. The helmsman has therefore to stand outside the cabin in order to steer. Of course this makes it a solitary job and one that requires you to be out in all weathers.

On the traditional narrow boat the sides of the boat are extended forwards from the engine room allowing further accommodation within. Another distinctive feature of this style of boat is the foredeck. This is large, as with the cruiser style, but is protected by another traditional feature – the cratch. On the old working boats this triangular structure held the tarpaulins and wooden planks above whatever cargo there was below. Nowadays, it's an attractive part of the boat, normally painted in a traditional diamond pattern and, with a cratch cover over it, protects the occupants from the weather if necessary.

The actual shape of the hull of a traditional narrow boat has been and is still often a bone of contention amongst boat

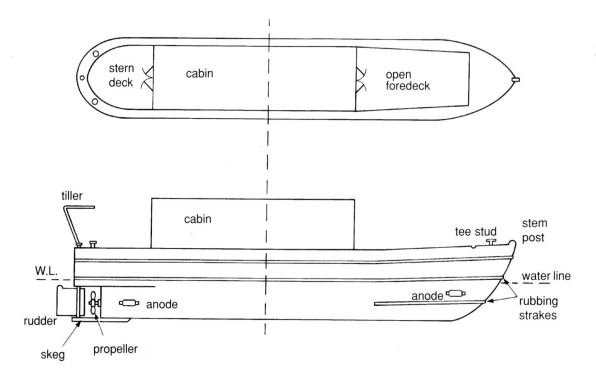

Modern narrow boat – cruiser style.

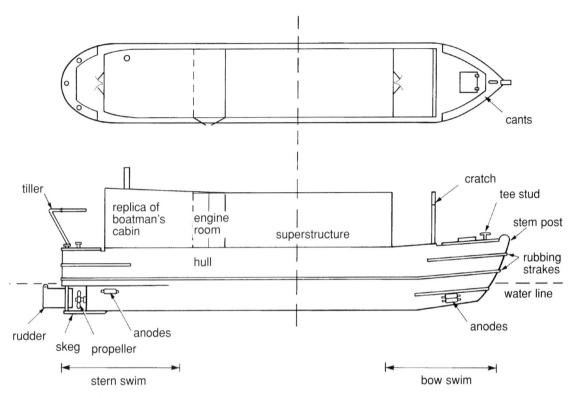

cants

cratch

tee stud

tiller

stem post

replica of
boatman's
cabin

engine
room

superstructure

rubbing
strakes

hull

water line

rudder

anodes

anodes

skeg   propeller

stern swim

bow swim

Modern narrow boat based on traditional lines.

*A traditional-style
narrow boat with
short deck. Room for
one at the tiller and
maybe one on the
gunwale for
company!*

builders. Some folk believe that a boat can only be termed traditional if it is several years old and is still capable of carrying cargo. That seems reasonable on the face of it, but the majority of narrow boats using the canal system today have been built with leisure use very much in mind and there has to be a reinterpretation of traditional styles to cater for what modern usage is proving to be.

Therefore, for the most part modern traditional-style narrow boats are adaptations of the old-style working boats, adhering as strictly as possible to those original designs whenever it can be sensibly achieved. I believe that the traditional style, when carefully planned and constructed for the individual, cannot be beaten for overall appearance, and that the judicial use of roses, castles and other forms of suitable decoration can transform the boat into an excellent

A modern replica of a working tug. The bow design here is one of David Baugh's from Black Country Narrowboats. He is one of a number of boat builders in the Black Country and surrounding area who construct BCN-replica tugs.

representation of what traditional narrow boating is all about.

The Josher Style

It doesn't end there though. The old Fellows, Morton and Clayton company back at the end of the last century wanted a style of boat which, while of course still being the usual working boat style, would best cater for their needs. Horse-drawn craft needed to be able to move through the water cleanly and smoothly; so was born the Josher style with its long swim of the stern and bow up to 14ft in length, and the graceful structure of the bows themselves sweeping upwards. The swim of the boat as it glided along the water was superb and the boats satisfied all concerned. They certainly met all the company's requirements.

When boats were converted to steam power and then eventually to diesel engines, considerable modifications had to be made to house the engine itself and the propeller, but the long swim was retained, once again giving a very pleasing overall effect and an important variation on the traditional theme.

The Tug Style

Another type of narrow boat to be seen on the canal system is the tug style, which were most common originally on Black Country canals. In the old days they were used for hauling trains of dumb coal boats, or Joeys, around the West Midlands. Normally they were not purpose-built but rather adaptations of obsolete horse-drawn craft cut down to cater for a motor-boat stern and, as was

A modern working tug replica of Jonathan Wilson design.

A pair of empty 'butties' lying adjacent to the tug James Loader. The riveted construction of the butties can be clearly seen.

Semi-traditional styles of narrow boat extend the cabin sides toward the stern, giving more protection for steering and more chance for companionship.

A selection of fibreglass and GRP cruisers; their range of design is as varied as that of more traditional narrow boats.

necessary years ago, a really big engine. The remnants of the hold were decked over in front of the engine room. Some purpose-built tugs were made in a similar style but with extended bow and stern swims.

Nowadays, tug-style narrow boats are similar to the traditional style but with the foredeck level with the gunwales and no cratch. You will see more and more of this style of narrow boat on the canal system. They look very interesting indeed, rather more unusual and, with a considerable amount of brasswork incorporated within their structure, very smart.

The Semi-Traditional Style

On the face of it you would think that was that when it came to narrow boat style, but no! A boat builder decided it would be a good idea to combine a number of features from the different types already available and produced what was termed a semi-traditional boat. This was an amalgamation of the advantages of the cruiser style with the very satisfying shape of the traditional style. It was largely achieved by enclosing the aft deck, where the boatman's cabin would have been, and covering the deck with a sliding

A Norfolk Broads-style hire cruiser. Boats such as this often introduce boaters to the joys of the inland waterways.

hatch or leaving it open, according to individual requirements.

These then are the styles that you can see regularly on the canal system. Internally the boats normally reflect the external style. It's up to you to decide what best meets your needs, bearing in mind the restrictions such narrow-beam craft have to abide by. But you don't always have to think narrow on the canal system, by any means! There are specifically built broad-beam steel boats now available in increasing numbers. Dutch barges, I suppose, are normally considered for use on rivers and wide canals such as the Grand Union. Basically, they are just less than double the width of the narrow boat at 13ft, but just think of the ways this extra width can be utilized!

Inland Motor Cruisers

Having dealt with the steel craft to be found and appreciated on the inland waterways system it's time to move on to

A modern GRP Wilderness cruiser providing comfortable cruising in a vessel of trailable dimensions.

GRP (glass-reinforced plastic) or fibre-glass inland cruisers. They are the most numerous sort of boat to be seen on the canals, being far more common than steel, but on the other hand they may be quite a few years old. The heyday of inland cruiser building was in the 1970s and early 1980s, when vast numbers of boats were produced, coinciding with the very successful canal restoration schemes during that time.

The main advantage of the lighter, more easily manoeuvrable inland cruisers is that they are considerably cheaper in price. A second-hand inland cruiser in good condition will often prove to be the ideal starter boat for newcomers to the canal system. The mind's eye might well be set eventually on a steel narrow boat of one of the types described above, but to many folk an inland cruiser is the passport to getting afloat and that is what it all boils down to in the long run.

When it comes to buying a new GRP cruiser constructed specifically for inland waterways, the companies in existence providing this service nowadays are far fewer in number than in those halcyon days of the 1970s. On the other hand, the construction today naturally uses the latest methods of manufacture and the most up-to-date equipment, and it achieves a quality of finish that will in many cases far surpass that which would have been available then.

New ideas and designs behind the construction are obviously going to be reflected in the cost price of such boats and all these factors have to be carefully weighed up when considering purchase. Check the boat tests and reports that appear in the inland waterways press on a regular basis and see whether the boats being written about come up to your expectations. Visit boat shows and waterways festivals and view as many boats as you can before coming to a decision. All boat builders are competing with one another for your order, in steel or GRP, and more than ever before there is a standard of craftsmanship throughout the canal system that is absolutely amazing.

Study the advertisements in the waterways press, send off for further information on the styles of craft you are searching for, speak to someone who knows what they're talking about and get the best advice you can – *before* you buy.

— 3 —

Buying a Boat

That first initial step into the world of inland waterways boating may on the face of it present a few problems. Not realizing in the first place that there was such a variety of craft from which to choose could bewilder the unwary, but most available boats fall into the two basic styles – narrow boat and inland cruiser – and if you are contemplating buying a boat it is in this area you will concentrate your attention.

The Right Boat for You

Family boating, living aboard, couple cruising or solo – your requirements will be reflected in the boat you choose. Cost

A smartly turned out inland cruiser looks good on any waterway. This one is on the Lee & Stort Navigation near the newly restored Waltham Town Locks.

is also of extreme importance. Second-hand (brokerage) or brand new boats will cover the full spectrum of prices and you are not going to be able to judge until you have had the chance to make some direct comparisons.

Reading the waterways press will not only give you some idea of what is available but will also indicate how quality and standard of fit-out can vary from one boat builder to another. You will know what sort of money you have to spend but you might also want to consider contacting a finance company for additional cash. This aspect is likely to depend on your collateral and status, but not always; it's certainly worth checking with individual finance companies to see what they have to offer. Companies who are advertising in the waterways press are obviously keen to be closely involved in marine finance. They will therefore be interested to hear of any propositions you have concerning your plans for the future.

Your ability to pay may only be half the consideration. Purchasing a steel hull or GRP hull for do-it-yourself fit-out could dramatically reduce the amount of money involved in the transaction. You will come across a number of boat builders who are keen to provide this sort of package, for example, taking the construction up to a certain point and then providing the plans, advice and materials for you to finish the job. It could well be that there are facilities available within the boatyard itself for you to carry on doing this, with just a minimal charge, which in addition gives full access to the right gear. DIY is now more popular than ever and it's definitely worth getting any literature you can referring to fitting out your own boat, or reading articles in the magazines which should give you loads of information.

Not everyone, of course, is quite so practically minded and skilled with their hands and for them the DIY option would never come into consideration. Full narrow boat or inland cruiser fit-outs are very time-consuming and time might not be available, especially if you want to start boating as soon as possible.

Study the classified advertisements in the waterways press to see what is available at the time. Some include a photograph of the boat for sale with details of what is on offer. The phone number at the end will give you the means of direct contact with the person selling the boat. The time of the month you buy the appropriate edition of the magazine may be an indication, however, as to whether it is still available or has already been sold. If you take out a subscription to a waterways magazine you will receive it several days before it appears in the shops and could well get first bite of the cherry – this option could be worth considering.

You'll also see larger advertisements giving lists of boats for sale in what are known as brokerage ads. There are some companies, often connected with boatyards or marinas, who specialize in selling second-hand boats for individual owners. They take away the responsibility for a percentage of the cost price, and ensure that as many potential boat buyers as possible are aware of the existence of these boats. Obviously, you don't get very much indication of what condition boats are in from just a few cursory phrases so I would recommend actually visiting a brokerage boatyard to examine the boats that attract your attention.

What to Look For

Let the boatyard know you are coming and which boat(s) you wish to view. Give them an approximate time of arrival so that they will be able to give you the time

Inland cruisers at moorings on the Stratford Canal. Many of these have long ceased to be manufactured but have been well maintained by their owners and are frequently available on brokerage sales.

age of the boat. Often the older a GRP craft is the more 'tired' the boat looks. Osmosis – the blistering that may be present on such boats – can indicate how well the boat has been looked after. Another point to consider with older boats is the Certificate of Compliance. The older the boat, the less likely it is to have one, so it's certainly worth checking. The Certificate is important as it will indicate that sufficient safety checks have been carried out on the boat, making sure it is completely canal- and river-worthy.

There will be a number of things to look out for inside the boat. The general condition, the windows, the electrics, the furnishings (those which have been retained) and certainly not least, the engine, will all have to be checked carefully. If possible get the engine running and check for sound levels and exhaust emission. Outboard engines may well have seen better days and it's not always possible to tell how old it is. If you do decide to go ahead and actually buy the boat it will need to be surveyed by a qualified marine surveyor. He will know exactly what it's all about and should be able to allay any initial fears or queries you might have.

necessary to discuss the boat and answer the questions you are bound to have. Brokerage boats will either be on the water or on the hard stand. The advantage with the latter is that you can closely examine the outside of the hull below the water line. You will be able to check the condition of the steelwork and the quality of the paintwork. A deterioration in either will be reflected in the price and in this instance it is very much a question of how much money you have to spare and what you are prepared to accept.

On an inland cruiser the quality of the fibreglass will depend very much on the

Buying New

Buying a brand new boat is going to be far more of a commitment than buying second hand and therefore needs to be planned very carefully beforehand. Scanning those boat builder advertisements and reading reports of their previous work should prove invaluable, but you need to get as much information before you as possible from a good cross-section of companies so that comparisons, where necessary, can be made.

Fortunately, nowadays, the competition being engendered within the inland boat building market is encouraging some superb craftsmanship. I never cease to be amazed by the standard of quality now to be seen from canal boat builders from all over the country. The use of fine wood finishings and careful design combined with top-quality equipment throughout the boat can transform the bare interior of the hull into something special. Many builders adapt the boat buyer's ideas within the overall style but on occasion these builders do prefer to adhere to their usual presentation and format. For some builders the style with which they have had proven success and experience over the years is the one they want to stick with. New boat builders on the scene may have very different ideas from the yards where they were trained perhaps, and it's interesting to see what can be achieved in the relatively confined space inside a narrow boat.

Another point to bear in mind concerns the credentials of the boat builder and whether he will actually come up with the finished boat in the end. Such question marks against a boat builder's credibility are unfortunate but there have been a few instances over the years where deposits have been put down and regular stage payments made and these funds have not been directed towards building the boat for the buyer, as the buyer intended. A way round this would seem to be careful recording of each stage of completion corresponding with the appropriate payment; this would be confirmed both by letter and personal visit to the yard. Check the contract before you sign it and ensure that the boat builder sticks to it.

The right gear for your boat. The choice is amazing and there is bound to be something to suit your requirements.

He will, at the outset, have given you some idea of when you can expect final completion and delivery. This date will be determined by the size of the operation and you should be able to plan ahead accordingly.

Happily, the majority of canal boat builders are honest people who love their work and love the inland waterways.

All the Extras

It is definitely worth getting one of British Waterways' Starter Packs to guide you through the boat-buying process. This contains all the details you need to know about licence fees (every boat must have a licence), mooring fees and insurance. Buying a boat can be a fairly expensive exercise on occasion and you have to be aware of all the additional costs that can be involved. The length of your boat will dictate how much your licence will cost, as will the location of your moorings. The quality of facilities you require can make the mooring fees fluctuate considerably.

Not all inland waterways are owned by British Waterways. You need to check who does own the navigation on which you are intending to be based: it is to them that you will need to direct your correspondence and appropriate payment. The National Rivers Authority (NRA) or individual Canal Trusts are responsible for the upkeep of their stretches of water, and the rates that they charge can vary considerably.

Some of the points I have mentioned might suggest that buying a boat is a daunting task. It's not. It is only if you are not fully *au fait* with what might go wrong, and how to act accordingly, that you could encounter difficulties. Joining the thousands of other inland waterway boaters on an ownership level can be a very satisfying experience. You may have fallen in love with canal and river boating when you first started to hire holiday cruisers and narrow boats; you'll absolutely adore it if you have the opportunity to become a boat owner!

— 4 —

Cruising Along

You're in charge! Once at the tiller of a narrow boat the inland waterways are yours to explore.

Before You Start

You've arrived at the boatyard. Before you cast off it is important that you:

1. Check that the boat isn't cluttered with empty cases. If you came in a car you should leave them in it.
2. Check that you've left details of your whereabouts in case of emergency. Even though you're on the move you can be traced if you leave the name of your boat, and the boatyard you hired it from, with contacts at home.
3. Check that the key to your boat – and any other small object you would hate to lose – will float. An empty plastic lemon makes an excellent key ring.

4. Ensure that two members of the crew (at least) know the rudiments of handling the boat. Then if the steerer falls in, someone else can take over and stop the boat.

5. Check the drill for 'man overboard'. Put the engine into neutral first (to remove the undertow from the propeller) and do not put the boat into full reverse until you have checked that the victim is clear of the propeller.

6. Bring your mooring pins back on board before you move on.

7. You must have an anchor if you are travelling on a river for the whole or part of your holiday. Rivers have currents and, in the event of a breakdown, could carry you where you do not wish to go.

All on top: the cabin roof is home for the boat hook, pole, plank and mop – all within easy reach.

8. Check your technique for dealing with flotsam. Speed up, then put the engine into neutral to glide over any rubbish until it appears astern.

9. Should your boat start losing speed or the engine overheats, check that your propeller is not fouled. If it is, try to lose the obstruction by reversing for short bursts, two or three times if necessary. Otherwise pull in, stop the engine, remove the weedhatch cover (on an inside engine) or pull up the outboard, and remove it. Remember the boat will flood if you don't replace the hatch securely.

10. Have you done your daily boat check? (Boats don't usually have gauges.) Check the engine oil level, the fuel tank level and the distilled water in the battery. If a diesel engine runs out of fuel the system will need professional attention before it can run again.

11. Have you read, in careful tranquillity, all the instructions on the boat regarding its handling and the equipment? Have you complained if there aren't any – written or verbal – or if they are insufficient?

So now you're ready. You've checked everything. You know where you're going. You know the route to take in order to get there. You're on the boat. And by no means least, you've got all the crew on board to help you on the way.

The start of a cruise is, I find, one of the most exciting parts of the whole trip: full of enthusiasm, the prospect of a week or so away from it all, just a touch of trepidation and anticipation about what you are going to encounter. This applies regardless of whether you have cruised the waterway before or not. If you are on a hire boat you should already have some idea of how she handles as there will have been a preliminary test drive to get you used to the controls. If it is your own boat you will have gained the boat-handling techniques from

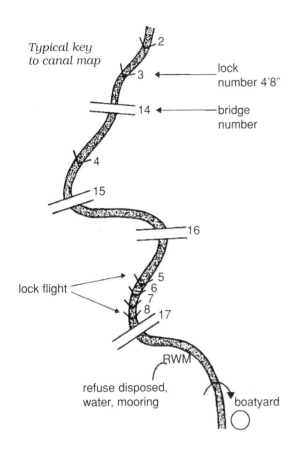

Typical key to canal map

lock number 4'8"

bridge number

lock flight

RWM

refuse disposed, water, mooring

boatyard

kept, not only by you but by the crew as well. Steady as she goes is the name of the game, but always remember that you need to have enough power to give you full control at all times. Allowing the engine just to tick over with the throttle in neutral once you have set off is not going to give you very much room for manoeuvre when trying to steer to where you want to go. Therefore, an occasional surge on the throttle clearly indicated by the churning of the propeller will ensure that you are always in charge of your boat at this early stage.

If other boats are also in the process of setting off, try to give some indication of when you are planning to make your move or wait until your stretch of waterway is clear. Frequently, getting out onto the main canal will involve some sharp turns and deft handling of the tiller arm. No matter how many times you've been out on a narrow boat, the response you get from your boat by moving the arm from left to right will fill you with a sense of achievement. No matter how long your boat is, as you stand at the stern with your hand on the tiller, the direction of movement will change very quickly in reaction to the slightest touch.

With the arm over to the left the boat will turn to the right, and similarly with the arm over to the right the boat will turn to the left. With this always in mind you will soon forget all about the normal steering of the wheel of the car and how that vehicle reacts! The response that an individual boat gives to the tiller will also depend on how much power the engine is emitting at the time. A slower speed will mean a slower reaction, and vice versa. As you play with the tiller arm in the early stages of your cruise you will soon ascertain the amount of 'swing' needed from side to side in order to achieve the required reaction from the boat.

previous experience. Even so, this experience can be very variable, ranging from a lot of time on the boat to only a minimal amount.

Leaving the Moorings

The correct way to move off from the moorings very much depends on where those moorings are. If they are within the confines of a boatyard or marina it's very likely that you will have to run onto the main waterway before you can really get going. There are bound to be lots of other craft about so a careful look-out has to be

Linear cruiser moorings – some boats are obviously used more often than others.

Careful manoeuvring when setting off. With the tiller arm well over to the right the boat responds with a sharp left turn.

The Canal Itself

Water Depth

In an ideal inland waterways system, the depth of water in the canals would be uniform throughout! The canals were manmade and excavated to allow the passage of boats but of course there is always going to be silting up to a greater or lesser extent. The deepest part of the waterway will always be in the centre with the depth decreasing as you move towards either bank. This V-shape is characteristic of all waterways and if you are not aware of it before you set off, you soon will be once your boat is moving.

The 'rule of the waterway' – to steer on the starboard (right-hand) side – is technically always applicable but in practice is mainly restricted to when you are passing another boat coming in the opposite direction. When there are no other oncoming boats to deal with immediately, it's best to keep in the middle of the canal. With the greater depth of water there your boat is always going to benefit. You will soon be aware of the speed of your boat, not only from what is registered on the display panel but from the amount of wash that is being created on the canal bank on either side. The size of your boat and the volume of water that it displaces within the canal will be clearly seen as the level of the canal lowers as you approach and resumes its normal level as you pass. The return of the water to its normal level and how quickly this is achieved is the 'wash' to which I refer.

The speed limit on the canal system is 4 miles an hour. This should be indelibly printed on your brain. Exceeding this speed will create a greater wash, which will be sufficient actually to cause erosion of the canal bank as the wash wave breaks. This form of erosion adds to the silting up of the waterway, creating lack of depth – the depth that is so necessary to ensure your boat's easy passage. In addition, if you exceed the speed limit when passing other moored boats, your wash will cause several problems, creating much movement of the boats against the canal bank and each other; and just spare a thought for those crew members on such a boat who might be enjoying a sit-down meal!

Among the equipment located on the roof of your narrow boat there should be a pole about 8–10ft (2.5–3m) in length. This is a very useful and necessary boating accessory on canals, and is used when you encounter a rather shallow stretch of waterway, normally towards the sides, where you might get stuck. By holding the pole about two-thirds of the way up its length and pressing the base of the pole against a firm surface, you can usually dislodge the boat from its shallow location on the mud. Combining this with deft use of the throttle will enable you to get free and back into deeper water. The

Cruising along – here on the Monmouthshire & Brecon Canal in South Wales.

firm surface creating the pressure to pole your boat off is vital. A soft surface where the pole itself can actually become stuck can end up with you losing your balance, as you will overstretch yourself if the boat moves. Sensible use of the boat pole, making sure that you control it and it doesn't control you, will mean that a shallow part of the canal can be negotiated very easily.

Meanderings

Referring to your canal guide should become second nature as you proceed with your cruise. Straight stretches of waterway will normally be interspersed with locks (discussed in Chapter 6) but some canals were built to follow the contours of the land, which avoided the building of locks but which did necessitate lots of bends and corners. Such meanders of the canal add to the interest factor in a canal cruise but at the same time demand greater concentration from the person at the tiller! There are a number of canals which twist and turn in such fashion – the Oxford Canal and the Monmouthshire & Brecon Canal to name but two.

If the narrow boat you are steering is less than 40ft in length then a bend in the canal should create no problems whatsoever. If your boat is longer than this then corners need to be negotiated more carefully. Once again the guidebook should give you some indication of the cruising scenario so that you know just what to expect. However, at a speed of 4 miles an hour, corners, no matter how tight they may be, are very straightforward. They can become a little more complex, though, if for example there happens to be a bridge on the bend to be negotiated at the same time!

Bridges

One side of the canal on which you are cruising will be privately owned by the local landowner. On the other side will be the towpath, usually owned by British Waterways. It will be on this side of the canal that you will normally moor up (discussed in Chapter 5) and in the days when horses were the only method of moving a boat it was from the towpath that the horses pulled.

Bridges carrying roads, lanes, farm tracks, footpaths and so on over the canal had to be built allowing for the towpath, but to save building materials – bricks or stone blocks – the canal narrowed at this point with the towpath, most often, passing under the bridge as well. As you approach such a bridge, whether it be on a corner or a straight stretch of canal, you will soon appreciate that going through a bridge hole requires a certain amount of concentration! If you are in the centre of the canal heading towards the bridge make sure you line your boat up as you get nearer and avoid approaching at an angle. Appearances can be quite deceptive when trying to judge whether you are on line or not, but a useful tip to remember is that the edge of the towpath, or the arch of the bridge as it enters the water, should be parallel to the sides of your boat. If it is parallel your boat will pass through the bridge hole without touching the sides, allowing for three or four inches between your near side and the bridge or towpath edge.

If you enter the bridge hole at an angle and you haven't lined up your boat sufficiently then you will not go through as smoothly. You are likely to touch the side to a greater or lesser extent and a member of your crew is likely to say something appropriate or give you a knowing look! Everybody does it from time to time so

The Oxford Canal, here at Aynho, narrows considerably when going under the bridge.

Lining up the boat prior to the bridge hole, making sure that the side of the boat is parallel to the edge of the towpath.

don't think you have committed a heinous crime if you encounter the nudge and ricochet syndrome! It's just nice to be able to pass through a bridge hole with confidence and return that knowing look to your crew!

Cruising on broad and narrow canals, you will encounter different types of bridge, but whatever kind they are they each present the steerer with a challenge and if, as mentioned above, they are on a bend in the canal, the challenge is even greater. It's worth giving a blast on the hooter if your visibility at the bend/bridge is impaired, thus letting any boat approaching from the other side know of your existence. If, when nearing the bridge, you can see that on the other side of it another boat is approaching, make a rapid judgement about who is the nearer

to the bridge. The nearest boat will have right of way to negotiate the bridge hole first and it is common courtesy to slow down and move over to allow him to do so. A mad rush to get there first is definitely not the way that it's done!

Lift and Swing Bridges

Not all bridges, of course, are permanent edifices that have to be tackled in the aforementioned fashion. Canals have always been adaptable and lift and swing bridges are great examples of this adaptability. However, encountering such a bridge by road is very different to doing so by water. It is the responsibility of the boater to work them properly if he wishes to make further progress. I have referred earlier to the importance of the towpath side of the canal as a means of access on

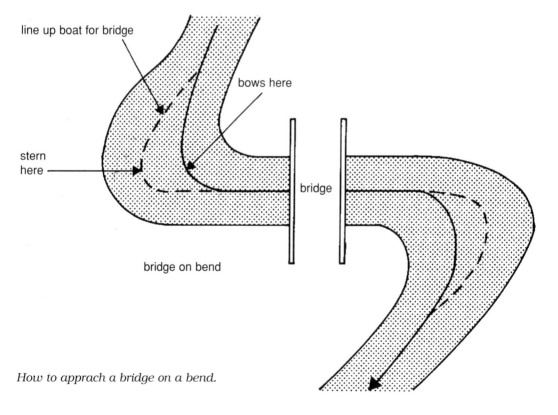

How to approach a bridge on a bend.

Narrow boats on the River Avon negotiate Welford Bridge. The right-hand arch is arrowed on the bridge itself indicating the correct way through.

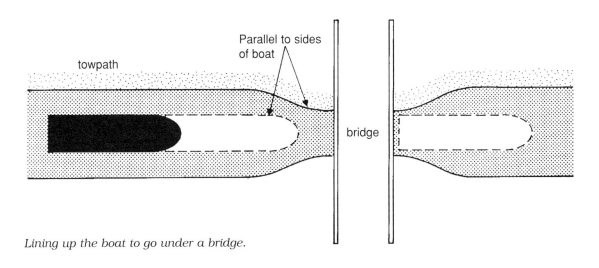

Lining up the boat to go under a bridge.

and off but, as luck would have it, all the working parts of swing and lift bridges are located on the opposite side!

A little bit of thought has to go into the best way to approach either type of bridge. If it is closed as you approach it's going to have to be opened; your boat will have to pass through; and it will then have to be closed again behind you. These are pretty obvious statements but easier said than done on occasion. Initially you are going to have to moor just before the bridge and let a member of your crew off to do the necessary business. Many such bridges, whether lift or swing, are worked by the same windlass or lock key that you use to operate locks, so remember to take it if you are the person responsible. Matters can be a bit more awkward if you are boating on your own (see Chapter 9).

Some of the lift bridges on the system need a bit of strength to set them in motion so perhaps this is not a job for the lightweights of your crew. Before any movement of either type of bridge you must check the state of traffic, if any, on the road at either side of the canal and bring the barriers down accordingly when there seems to be a pause in the flow of cars. Some of the swing bridges on the Leeds & Liverpool Canal carry busy roads across the waterway and they can be rather stiff to move as well. But normally it's a straightforward operation, merely requiring basic common sense.

More and more bridges, of both types, are being adapted as hydraulic or electrified. You will need your British Waterways key with you to open the box of tricks by the side of the bridge, within which you will find full instructions on how it works. Follow these carefully and press the buttons in the right order and you should have no problems at all. Granted, they are far easier to work than their manual counterparts, but then again if you yearn for canal boating of the traditional variety then electrified lift and swing bridges don't quite fall into this category. It's all a question of attitude and preference, I suppose, and as with all cruising on the inland waterways you have to take the rough with the smooth – and it is nice to have some smooth bits now and again!

A newly restored lift bridge, such as this, is a pleasure to operate – but don't be fooled into thinking they are all that easy!

A lift bridge ahead means that someone has to jump off to operate it while you get ready to take the boat through when it is open.

Another challenge – this time a lift bridge operated by using the windlass for the hydraulic mechanism.

Photographed from the road below, this is impressive Edstone Aqueduct on the Stratford Canal.

The majestic Pontcysyllte Aqueduct carring the Llangollen Canal over the River Dee – which flows a mere 150ft or so below!

Aqueducts

From time to time during your cruise, although not on every waterway by any means, you're going to come across aqueducts in some form or other. For the most part you are hardly going to be aware that you are or have passed through one. Aqueducts carry water within the canal over a road, river or another waterway, and are used to obviate the need for a canal junction. Some aqueducts are far from insignificant. They can be major features on the waterway and it is very obvious indeed that you are passing over one. The Pontcysyllte Aqueduct on the Llangollen Canal is undoubtedly the most dramatic on the system and channels the waterway more than 150ft (45m) above the River Dee.

The aqueduct itself, as far as the canal is concerned, is a narrow trough of water, slightly wider than your boat. Steering your boat carefully through this trough can demand considerable concentration and positive thinking. If you are not over-keen on heights it is best to keep your eyes firmly ahead on the canal itself. Windy weather conditions can add to your problems as you tend to approach in crab-like fashion; but once you have mastered your first aqueduct you will never feel that same apprehension again, I can assure you. That doesn't mean to say that you are going to become blasé about them; they always have to be treated with respect.

You will come across aqueducts on several parts of the system and your guidebook should give a good indication as to where these are and when you are going to encounter them. Like all challenges, however, you will feel a warm glow of satisfaction when you have successfully negotiated them!

Up at canal level the narrow trough, with the towpath on one side, is often exposed to gusty winds, so concentration is required when navigating.

Into the Darkness

The other major feature you will encounter on many waterways is the tunnel, burrowing its way through the hillside to avoid the necessity of having to build flights of locks, and allowing a more direct route to the final destination. Tunnels are quite incredible feats of engineering. For the most part they were built up to 200 years ago when methods of construction basically consisted of primitive

Negotiating the Pontcysyllte Aqueduct – a memorable experience.

A tunnel safety sign located shortly before a tunnel entrance. It's not always possible to absorb the information on it fully while on the move, but it is basic common sense.

The headlight of a narrow boat situated at the bow, of course. Switch it on before entering the tunnel and switch on the cabin lights as well for more illumination.

spades and wheelbarrows.

All tunnels have their own individuality and vary in size and length according to the particular hillside they have to negotiate. As you, the boater, approach a tunnel you will already know the length from your guidebook and also, of course, whether it is broad or narrow. Towards the entrance of either tunnel portal you cannot help but see a British Waterways notice, listing a number of points to note to ensure your safe passage. These points might be a bit difficult to absorb in so

short a time but, as with most obstacles, getting over them is mainly a matter of using your common sense.

Narrow tunnels will have a tunnel keeper at the end who will let you know how the one-way traffic system is progressing and when it is your turn to go. There will also be a tunnel gauge on the smaller tunnels to give you some indication of the minimum height, in parts. Clear the roof of any gear that might be swept off and in particular remember your chimney(s). You don't want to lose

The unusual entrance to Shrewley Tunnel on the Grand Union Canal. Note the tunnel has its own towpath tunnel on the right and slightly above.

This tunnel entrance – to Dudley Tunnel – photographed a few years ago, looks somewhat daunting.

A narrow boat approaches and enters Shrewley Tunnel. The headlight is on and the crew at the stern are wearing waterproofs. Some tunnels are exceptionally moist so be prepared.

those. Switch on your headlight before entering the tunnel; sometimes it's a good idea to switch on the lights inside the boat as well. This will help to illuminate your journey. Get the crew inside so only the steerer is out on the rear deck.

Tunnels on broad canals are certainly less claustrophobic and in the main you can stick to the middle as you cruise along. You will certainly be aware of an approaching boat as the headlight gets nearer and nearer, although this is often very deceptive and it's difficult to judge where other boats are until they are almost on top of you. Stay to the right as you pass. It can be quite deafening with the noise of two engines at once in the close confines of the tunnel, but this is always an exhilarating experience.

It's also worth remembering that quite a few tunnels are very 'drippy', with water cascading down in large dollops on occasion. A waterproof jacket is therefore a must. The eerie half moon of light at the bow of your boat will pick up the downpourings of water and you should be able to judge quantity and force and be prepared for it by the time you make your return journey!

The majority of tunnels, however, are 'dry' and short – just a few hundred yards in length. You can see the other end approaching quite clearly and if, like me, you normally have quite a vociferous crew, there is a hearty cheer when you are once more out in the daylight. That's when you can look back at the retreating portal, grin and say to yourself, 'no problem'!

— 5 —
Manoeuvres

Moving Off

It may have been just a short-term mooring to buy a few essentials at a nearby shop or an overnight stop-off after a day spent cruising – for whatever reason your boat has been tied up, you are going to want to set off again eventually.

Where you actually moored in the first place is going to affect how you approach your leaving. If the boat is tied up to a canal bank and adjacent to the towpath, with no other boats in the vicinity, then it's going to be pretty straightforward. Always check behind you to see if there are boats nearby that wish to pass. If you are just setting off you will be travelling fairly slowly so your manoeuvrability will be affected. It's better to be sure that the waterway is clear so you can get away from your moorings easily and efficiently.

Untying the ropes and removing the mooring stakes, if they have been used, will enable your boat to drift free from the bank; then, applying appropriate power from the engine, gradually bring the tiller arm over so the boat itself will respond. Narrow boats, however, are not the easiest of beasts to persuade into doing what you want them to! More likely than not you will find yourself dragging along the side making little or no leeway into the centre of the canal. It's a good idea to get a member of the crew to push you off at the bow end, so you are pointing out and in the right direction. There is no risk of the crew member being left behind as the

boat has hardly yet reached walking speed.

If you are approaching a bend in the canal and this is going to prove to be somewhat difficult, judicious use of the throttle, with some emphasis on reverse as well, will ease your boat out into the canal proper. If your boat has been moored in a line with quite a few other craft then your manoeuvrability will be more restricted. Furthermore, you may well have your neighbour's ropes attached to the same mooring ring or bollard and you may have to untie his ropes in order to get at yours. Whether this is a pain in the neck or creates no problems whatsoever depends on how you and your neighbour tied your ropes up in the first place.

Once you have freed your boat from its confines, a member of your crew will have to be co-opted to shove the boat out far more dramatically to give the engine greater capability of getting you out into the main canal. You always have to be wary of the stern end of the boat as narrow boats do cut corners, so once again, the tiller arm and rudder response will have to be brought into play. Once you are fully away from your mooring, tend to the ropes, coiling them neatly near to where they are attached to your boat. Then when you need them again they can be picked up easily and thrown in a coil to the crew member on shore.

Your mooring may well have been in a marina, where there is a variety of types

Not only good moorings here, but also water and electricity laid on. This is typical of many marinas and the facilities they provide nowadays.

of mooring that you will come across from time to time. Finger or pontoon moorings use the area of water available in far more concentrated a fashion. After all, the marina owner is always keen for as many boats as possible to use the facilities that he can provide. You may find, therefore, that getting away from the pontoon and steering your boat out of the marina and onto the canal will require some skilful manoeuvring – the amount and degree of difficulty once again depending on the length of your craft. Keep an eye open for other moored boats that may not have been tied up as well as yours (!) and also for signs indicating the way out of the marina. That's not as daft as it sounds. Concentrating on a number of factors all at once can mean that you overlook the obvious. Leaving a marina means just

that and does not require several laps of honour round the moorings as if you are loath to go!

Turning Round

During your cruise, especially if you are not undertaking a 'ring' circuit, there will come a time when you have to turn round and commence the return leg of your journey. Whether you have been travelling on a broad or a narrow canal, the actual width of the waterway will still impose restrictions on turning round. The longer your boat, of course, the more apparent the restriction will be.

Referring to your canal map or waterway guide you will see arrows, drawn in a 180-degree curve, at certain points along

Pontoon moorings, end on, allow plenty of craft to take advantage of the space available.

An intricate mooring system, such as this at Limehouse Marina on the Regent's Canal, takes some planning.

the canal. These indicate winding holes – pronounced 'wind' as in north, south, east or west wind – so called because in the days of purely horse-drawn boats the strength of the wind against the side of the barge helped to manoeuvre the boat round. A winding hole, I suppose, is like a lay-by cut into the canal side. This semi-circle of additional water space is there to help you turn your boat round. In an ideal world these winding holes would be kept dredged to a sufficient depth to ensure that their use causes no problems with boats getting stuck, but unfortunately their location is often such that

they soon become silted up, either from lack of use or because they are sometimes used by the local farmer's cows as a watering hole!

Check out the position of the winding hole in relation to locks and so on, and work out whether you will have to negotiate a few of these in order to use the former. It hardly seems worth it to go to all that trouble, especially if time is of the essence and there was a winding hole further back, which you passed earlier, which would have sufficed. There are some canal boaters, not including you of course, who categorically believe that

Making the approach with the winding hole on the right. Turn in when the bow of the boat can reach the centre, and fullest width, of the winding hole.

Head in at 45 degrees, watching your stern and allowing yourself as much space as possible.

By using forward and reverse gears, bring the boat round with the throttle so that it is at right angles across the canal.

Repeat the to and fro operation ...

... until you are facing the direction whence you came.

Nifty work on the tiller arm sees the boat round.

Of couse, sideways performance, with the use of a bow thruster, can speed up the whole scenario!

Negotiating a tight turn.

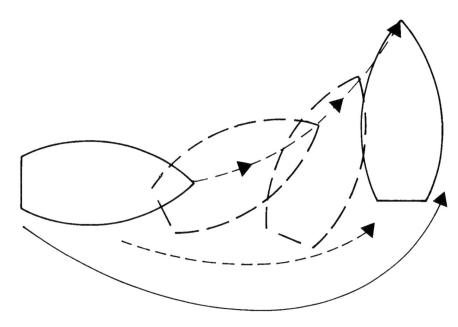

In a confined space, forward and reverse action will be necessary to accomplish a 90-degree turn.

winding holes are there to provide an excellent, trouble-free mooring! As soon as a boat, of whatever size, is moored up within a winding hole it immediately puts that winding hole out of action as it obviously prevents other boaters from using it. Similarly, if a boat is moored up exactly opposite a winding hole it will again stop it being used for its intended purpose. Therefore winding holes, when it comes to mooring, are 'no-go' areas. I sometimes think there ought to be a concerted campaign for the excavation of more winding holes. They never seem to be in the places you want them – but then again, if everything on the canal system was there in anticipation of what boaters wanted all the time, then there would be no individuality in your own cruising activities.

Approaching the winding hole itself once again requires checking of the canal for approaching craft: if all is clear you can start your manoeuvre. Steer the bow of the boat practically into the widest part of the canal created by the winding hole, allowing yourself just slightly more width to play with. Then by reversing and subsequently moving the boat backwards and forwards it should gradually begin to swing round until it is pointing in the direction from which you came. The number of individual movements that this requires before you achieve your goal will depend on the length of the boat; the shorter the craft the easier it will be, and conversely, the longer the craft, the longer the time it will take. It's still easy to do and it's far better to enter bow first than to reverse in. This is because the business end of your boat is at the stern with both the vital rudder and propeller being

Facilities en route – diesel pump, provisions, chandlery. Here at Aynho Warf on the Oxford Canal.

Linear moorings near Springfield Marina on the Lee & Stort Navigation. Note the range of boat types.

located here. If the winding hole has become somewhat silted up you certainly don't want them to be caught on the mud. It's much safer to have the stern end out in the canal where the deepest water is to be found.

Winding holes are an interesting local diversion on your cruise, which can provide the steerer with extreme satisfaction if negotiated properly and successfully, but extreme frustration if not! A bow thruster fitted to your boat can provide an easy way out of such a difficulty as you can direct the front of the boat sideways with just a press of a button, but some boaters feel that this is cheating yourself out of a challenge!

Stopping and Mooring Up

I dealt with setting off from your moorings at the beginning of this chapter and showed that this can be as straightforward as you wish to make it. Stopping the boat and mooring up requires more careful planning but need not prove too awesome. Having decided on where you are going to moor – you will probably have examined your map or guide which tells you where such sites are specifically located – you need to steer the boat over. Remember as you do this to keep the engine running at all times. As soon as you switch off the engine you will lose control of the boat. The momentum you

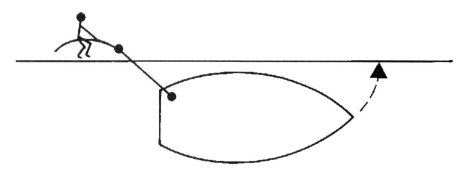

Stopping the boat with a stern rope.

had prior to reaching your mooring will be lost and the boat will appear to have a mind of its own, being affected both by wind and wash from other passing craft. Keep the engine running until you have actually tied up. Bring the bow in first, then bring the stern in by putting the tiller arm over away from the mooring. You can then put the throttle briefly into reverse to complete the job. Otherwise the crew member on the bank can help to pull you in. However, on a boat with an out-board engine you can turn the wheel towards the mooring and reverse. Doing this will bring the stern around.

When the nose of the boat is into the bank get someone to step off with the bow rope. Make sure you are close enough in to avoid making that step a leap into the unknown. What might appear to be a fair-ly narrow gap to someone steering the boat at the stern, might in actuality be a considerable distance for the person with the rope to hand. Once on the bank or

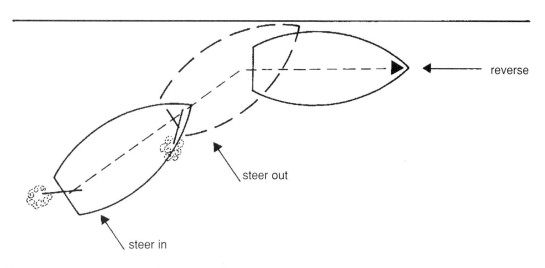

reverse

steer out

steer in

In order to turn to the left the stern must have room to swing to the right.

Equidistant mooring bollards not only provide a smart overall appearane but also security.

The rope from the T-mooring stud ensures the front part of the boat is securely tied.

towpath he can make the boat secure to either a mooring ring or a stake driven in with the lump hammer. Before this can be done, of course, you have to get the stern of the boat into the side as well. Throwing the rope from the stern would seem to be the obvious answer but check that the distance between the boat and the bank is not greater than the length of rope you have. If the gap is too wide, the rope will always fall in the water, no matter how well you have thrown it in the first place.

Coiling the rope, then holding it with one hand, and throwing it with the other is the best method. You can practise this beforehand till it becomes second nature. Otherwise you can guarantee that if you

are throwing a rope when people are watching from the towpath it will always fall in the water.

Mooring stakes, if needed, and the lump hammer used to drive them in, can be thrown out onto the grass before jumping off the boat. Mooring stakes are about 18in (45cm) in length and have a pointed end which goes into the ground and a blunt end for hammering. Place them beyond (rather than level with) the bow and stern of the boat to fasten the boat more securely into the bank. Hammer the blunt end driving, the stake into the ground at a 45-degree angle pointing away from the boat. If that angle is towards the boat there is a danger of the

Well set back from the canal itself these bollards were obviously intended for much larger craft. Tying up here could create problems with ropes lying across the towpath.

Not over-substantial, but a rope fender such as this will prevent the side of the boat from scraping against the wooden pontoon.

rope slipping off. If you hammer the stake in vertically there will be no additional support for it and the chances are when you return to your boat later the stakes will have worked out with the motion of passing boats and your own craft will have swung free. Sometimes boaters blame this on some idiot pulling them out. More often than not it will be their mistake initially in not checking.

A couple of half-turns with the rope around the stake will temporarily secure the rope and keep the boat itself in towards the canal bank. The rest of the boat can then be secured at the stern. It could well be that by this time the rear

will have started to swing out into the canal. All the more reason, therefore, to have your rope coiled up in advance ready for throwing to the crew member on the towpath.

A rope at the bow and another at the stern should be sufficient for an average-length narrow boat, remembering that there is little or no movement of water. But for peace of mind, if there is the possibility of boat movement from the wash of passing craft, a third rope can be used from the centre of the boat. Check that you have driven the mooring stakes in to a sufficient depth and that they are firm and don't wiggle about. The ground into

Bringing the rope back to the boat from the mooring post and returning it again, complete with additional hitch, improves an already secure mooring.

These moorings are on the approach to a lock at Teddesley on the Staffs & Worcs Canal. They are well laid out and blend in well in an attractive setting.

A combination of slip-way, pontoon and quayside moorings make this marina – Willowtree on the Southern Grand Union Canal – an ideal location.

which you hammer them may vary from being very hard to being exceptionally soft. You will therefore need to vary the depth of the stakes accordingly.

In addition, make sure that the stakes and the ropes are not strung out across the towpath where they can trip up the unwary and prove a considerable hazard. The top of the stake can be covered with a inverted empty plastic bottle to protect an unguarded ankle or shin and also to make it more visible. If you have been unable to manoeuvre your boat really close into the side – perhaps owing to lack of depth of water or to abundance of vegetation – you will probably have to lodge the boat plank between the gunwale and the bank itself. Again, check that this is firmly fixed and is not likely to drop off into the water.

There are many moorings available that do not require mooring stakes. There may be purposely placed bollards or mooring rings and in some areas, perhaps within a marina, there may even be someone there to help you tie up or to check you have done it properly. The section below on ropes and knots should give you a good idea as to which is going to be the best one for you to use as the situation arises.

Knowing the Ropes

The clove hitch is the best type of knot for tying up to a bollard. It is simple and easy to accomplish. Again, practising beforehand is a good idea. The knots illustrated on the next page are the ones most commonly used for canal and river cruising, so you must learn them and practise them till you are confident you can use

These excellent mooring cleats on a finger pontoon are very substantial, allowing plenty of rope to create the necessary security.

them. Boaters of long standing who have been doing it for years become very accomplished in knot tying and realize that doing it properly is an integral part of boating and boat handling.

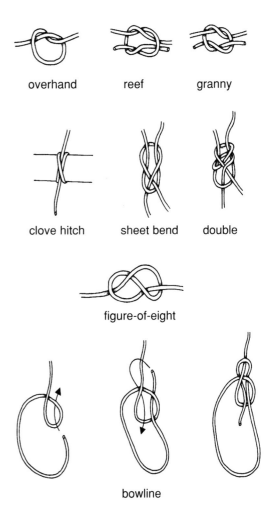

overhand   reef   granny

clove hitch   sheet bend   double

figure-of-eight

bowline

The Elementary Rules of Mooring

1. Come in bow, or nose, first.
2. Have a member of your crew standing ready at the bow to jump off with a rope to haul in the bow while you concentrate on the stern.
3. Do not switch off the engine until you are safely tied up.
4. Stay at the tiller and never leave it unattended.
5. Ensure that you have the correct lengths of rope: longer at the bow, shorter at the stern.
6. Drive your mooring stakes or pins in at an angle of 45 degrees, leaning away from the boat.
7. Always check the area around where you are intending to moor up and avoid aqueducts, viaducts, railway lines, busy motorways and potentially noisy pubs.

If you follow these suggestions you shouldn't go far wrong and as you become increasingly adept at mooring and tying up, you will have the satisfaction of knowing that the expertise you are gaining is part of becoming a successful inland waterways boater.

Some of the basic knots are pictured here; use the clove hitch for mooring to a bollard, the sheet bend for joining two ropes that aren't the same size, the figure-of-eight as a stopper knot, and the bowline for almost everything.

6

Locks

What Are They and Why?

Probably the one subject area that comes up more than any other when considering boating on the inland waterways is that of locks, those steps in the canal that raise and lower the water level of a canal across the countryside. I suppose if there is anything about inland cruising that causes apprehension, amongst new boaters in particular, it has to be locks. They are so variable, not only in size and type, but also in the way they are maintained. When you remember how old some of these structures are, it's remarkable that they are still in working order and that their basic simplicity has stood them in good stead for so long.

If you are contemplating boating on a particular waterway on which there are a number of locks it is recommended that you have a close look at the appropriate canal guide. Planning your route and deciding in advance where you intend to visit is always a sensible move; at the same time you should be able to ascertain exactly where the locks are located and what type they are. This will very much depend on whether the canal is broad or narrow and if the local terrain is basically flat, undulating or dramatically hilly. All canals are fed from a reservoir at the highest level (the summit) and the movement of water that enables the locks to be fed is naturally in a downwards progression either side of this summit.

If you look at a number of individual canal maps you should soon work out which part of the waterway is at the waterway's highest point and which is at its lowest. For example, if you are heading northwards on a canal from the starting point at its junction with another waterway you are more likely than not to be going uphill. Uphill in this respect means that each lock you encounter will be a step upwards as you progress. Individual locks vary in depth, according to their exact location in the surrounding landscape, but you will generally find that on any one waterway most or all of the locks you come across will be of the same type and will be operated in the same manner. Thank goodness for that! There would be some tremendous mix-ups if this were not the case.

Each section of the canal between locks is known as a pound. A long pound indicates, obviously, that there is a fair distance, maybe a few miles, between locks; a short pound, the opposite. After negotiating a number of locks in perhaps a short distance, a long pound is definitely appreciated. A break from lock-working makes one very much aware of the rest period in between!

Broad locks and narrow locks are to be found through the canal system. Those on the main lines – the major waterways – are normally going to be broad because the canals are broad. Those inter-linking waterways connecting cross-country routes with major centres are normally going to be narrow canals. You can soon

A narrow lock with a single lock gate. Only one boat at a time is allowed through in either direction. One of the most enjoyable locks to operate.

work out which is which by examining a map of the canal system, which will have a key showing the different types. Broad locks are capable of taking two boats abreast at a time whereas narrow locks can only take one boat at a time in either direction. It will take longer to operate a broad lock as a considerably greater volume of water is involved in its emptying and filling. On the other hand its narrow counterpart is going to take a lot less time – less water, only a single lock gate and only half the operation.

I like narrow locks. They seem to be far more user-friendly and cosier. Being quicker to work, the canal boater seems to make far more substantial progress without appearing to be stuck in the same place for what seems to be an eternity! On the other hand, if you're cruising on a broad canal with its broad locks it's always nice when you meet up with another boat going in the same direction at the same time. You can then halve the duties, or take it in turns. Of course, this depends on whether you hit it off straight away with your narrow boating colleague.

Wide double locks on the Lee & Stort Navigation. A centrally positioned lock-keeper is normally on duty to help you through.

Not everyone is going to be as nice and pleasant to be with as you are!

Approaching a Lock

The carefree manner of cruising along a lock-free stretch of waterway comes to an end as soon as the first lock comes in sight. Locks can be spotted from quite some distance as they are usually painted in black and white and stand out quite starkly from their surroundings. As you get nearer you should soon be able to judge whether the lock is empty or full. Depending on whether you are going up (towards the summit level) or not, you will either be able to enter straight away once you have opened the lock gates or you will have to prepare the lock.

If a member of your crew hops off onto the towpath, to check in advance as you approach, he will soon be able to let you know which is the case. If the water level has to be altered before you can enter then it is best to moor up before the lock.

Overflow channels or by-weirs just before a lock will allow excess water in the canal to pass by. The amount can vary considerably according to conditions.

Open lock gates at St Pancras Lock. If you are approaching from the north therefore you have direct access into the lock itself on this occasion.

You will normally find a mooring spot just before you reach the gates themselves, where you can tie up and get yourselves sorted out. Making sure you have your windlass or lock key with you, walk up to the lock and check out the situation. Your windlass is your only means of operating the lock as paddles have to be opened or closed to allow water in or out of the lock.

Operating the Lock

Nothing can be done until the lock gates at either end are shut. Creating the lock chamber by doing this enables you to control fully the movement of the water. When moving in an uphill direction it will be necessary to empty the lock if it is full to allow your boat to enter. By opening the paddles (usually just the ground paddles) using the windlass, the water will drain out of the lock until it is at the same level as you are. You will now be able to open the lock gates by putting your weight against the balance beams and the gates themselves will slowly open. A useful tip here is to remember that if you are operating a broad lock and there is only one boat – your own – in need of using it, it will only be necessary to open one gate. A narrow boat is designed to be able to negotiate one gate only. However, if your boat is of broader beam than usual then naturally both gates will have to be opened.

So with the gate(s) open the boat can be steered into the lock. If you have moored up to the side of the canal or kept the boat centrally positioned waiting for the lock operator to do his job, you need to make sure your boat does not enter the lock itself at an angle. Line it up so that you will be able to go in without knocking the sides against the lock gate or the lock wall. That's easier said than done, I know, and it will only be through the negotiating

of a number of locks and the experience gained as time goes on that you will get it right. The direction and strength of the wind will affect the boat and make it easy or difficult to handle efficiently.

Take it steady entering the lock. Gently take the boat through the open gates into the lock and pull in to the side of the lock wall. Ropes at the bow and stern of the boat should now be securely looped over the bollards usually found at the side of the lock. Pulling on the ropes will enable you or your lock operator to make sure the boat is kept steady within the lock and doesn't bang about when the water is let in, raising you and boat up to the next

Mitre gates on the Lee & Stort. Note the difference in the water level on either side.

A good example of the turbulence that can affect a lightweight inland cruiser in a wide lock. Tying up securely is imperative.

Paddle gear operated on lock gates themselves, operated by the normal windlass or lock key.

level. When you are satisfied your boat is secured against the lock wall and the lock gates behind you have been shut, the ground paddles can be opened, once again using the windlass. Another tip to remember is that a slight forward push on the throttle will produce enough wash from the propeller to push against the lock gate to keep it closed if it tends to want to open a little bit. Using the power of the water to hand to your advantage whilst operating a lock is something you will certainly learn to do as you gain more experience.

If the ground paddle is opened on the opposite side of the lock to the boat the influx of water into the lock will hold the boat against the wall. Many locks have

gate paddles as well but I would certainly not recommend opening those initially – wait until the level of water in the lock has risen considerably. The flow of water from gate paddles, especially if they have been fully opened, can be quite dramatic, and depending on the length of your boat and the proximity of the bow to the gate itself, it can mean that water can get into the bow well.

You will have noticed earlier when you brought the boat into the lock – remember I am referring to the lock in its empty state – that the lock gates themselves are pretty substantial structures built on a solid base to support their weight. This base is known as a cill or sill and of course is easily visible when the lock is in

A single narrow boat in a wide lock being held to the side with a centrally positioned rope.

its empty state. However, when the lock is full and you want to empty it to go down to the next level, be wary of the cill at either end. Position your boat within the lock as centrally as possible. Shorter craft will have no problem but a longer narrow boat using almost the full length of the lock will have to be handled carefully, adjusting the throttle as necessary if the boat encroaches towards the position of the cill. At some locks a line is painted beside the lock at each end indicating where the cill is found. Keep the boat inside these lines and you should have no problem at all.

Entering the lock from the opposite direction – going downhill – the method is the same except on this occasion the water is being emptied from the lock into the pound below rather than from the pound above into the lock. Making sure as before that the boat is tied up securely against the lock wall, let out the rope as the boat slowly sinks down to the lower level. Within a broad lock, duties can normally be halved if there is another boat to

A wide-beam cruiser being secured by looping the bow rope over a mooring post.

The ubiquitous cill on which the lock gates are built. Make sure the boat is beyond any possibility of being hung up or of catching its rudder on it.

Many locks leak water to a greater or lesser extent. It's best to keep the boat clear of the cill and any such leakage to prevent an ingress of water on board.

share the lock with you. Couple this with the fact that you are not likely to move about in the lock itself and you are saving water – a complete lockful – then a shared lock is pretty beneficial.

There is no sharing of course in a narrow lock! Prior to emptying or filling the lock, check to see if there are any boats approaching from the opposite direction. If the level of the water in the lock favours the boat coming towards you, you should wait until he arrives so that he can benefit from your disadvantage rather than wasting a whole lockful of water just so you can gain a few minutes overall.

Leaving the Lock

When the water has filled the lock you and your boat will be up on the same level as the canal ahead of you. The lock operator will be able to lean on the balance beam and it should move, thus opening the lock gate. If it is impossible to move then there is still a bit more water to enter the lock chamber to equalize the levels on either side of the gate. Another tip to bear in mind when opening the lock gate is always to push with your back rather than straining yourself pushing with your arms. There is usually some raised brick-

Share-a-lock. In a wide lock two narrow boats will make the rise or fall of water much more stable for each craft as well as, of course, saving water.

or stonework on the ground to give you a firmer foothold.

Once the lock gate is fully opened, close the paddle with the windlass. Never leave the windlass on the spindle whilst waiting for the lock to fill or empty. There is a catch which connects onto the ratchet preventing the paddles from dropping on their own accord – so make sure you use it! When lowering the paddles do it steadily, keeping your hand on the handle of the windlass. Letting the paddles fall under their own weight is a foolhardy thing to do and can also damage the mechanism of the lock for future users.

Back on the boat and you can untie the ropes from the bollards and slowly steer out of the lock. A final check that the paddles are shut and that you have closed the gates behind you, and you have completed the lock operation – always a satisfying achievement. Merely the thought of having just successfully (I hope!) negotiated a lock usually makes me feel pleased, particularly if a number of onlookers have been watching my every move! Gongoozlers, as they are known, often seem to me to be hoping that you will make some error which will cause you considerable embarrassment and make them smile!

Flights and Staircase Locks

Some sections of the canal will be moving up or down a slope for a considerable number of miles and this will mean that there will be a number of locks in fairly quick succession. Anything from four or five to forty or fifty locks can come all together. These are known as flights of locks and to the uninitiated may appear somewhat daunting. Tackling one lock after another can speed up the process of learning lock operating dramatically: they will practically become second nature! On the other hand you should have plenty of time and should not be in any particular

The bridge beyond the lock is on the same level as the lock itself. An excellent example of clever, and sometimes deceptive, canal architecture.

Part of the Knowle flight of locks on the Grand Union Canal in Warwickshire. They are of the very substantial and wide type and provide a challenge on the waterway.

rush to get to the next point along your route. Often you will come across a pub or hostelry en route where you can take a break. Some boaters, on the other hand, will just want to get them over and done with as soon as they can.

Once again a close examination of the guidebook will tell you if you are going to have to negotiate any lock flights. It is entirely up to the individual boater which canal route he chooses – one with many locks or one with fewer. However, I don't think you can consider yourself fully initiated into the art of canal boating until you have tackled every obstacle on the way. Flights of locks are part of the system and therefore have to be treated with respect and to the best of your ability.

Sometimes you will come across a steeper rise in the land through which the canal passes. In such places a flight of locks can be replaced with a lock staircase. This basically consists of a number of locks joined up with one another, one lock virtually leading into the next. You will find at the start of the staircase an instruction board by the towpath, which will give you details of how the locks ahead of you should be tackled. If you follow these instructions you should not go wrong. Remembering that the lockfuls of water have to move in one direction – either all up or all down – will ensure that you will always have sufficient for the requirements of your own boat. Only one boat at a time can negotiate a lock

On the Bascote staircase on the Grand Union Canal, where each lock loads into the next.

staircase so if there is someone already using the locks you will have to wait. This will give you time to learn those instructions by heart! They are actually pretty easy to follow, and after all it's only common sense that's needed!

Once again you should be aware from your canal guidebook when you're going to meet a lock staircase. The most famous must be the Bingley Five-Rise on the Leeds & Liverpool in West Yorkshire. This is actually a tourist attraction for non-boaters for miles around – in other words gongoozlers again! However, there is a lock keeper to help you at the locks so assistance is always at hand. Other staircase locks you can encounter are the Northgate locks at Chester and the Bunbury flight. Bascote on the Grand Union has a small flight of three locks, so it is a good one to practise on, but of course you have to get there in the first place!

Bingley Five-Rise locks on the Leeds & Liverpool Canal. The lock keeper will help you if confusion sets in amid the apparent complexity! And just look at all those gongoozlers!

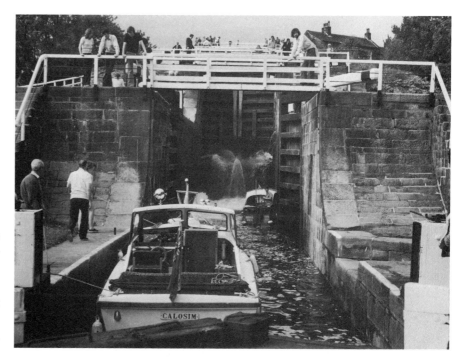

You'll Grow to Love Them!

The more locks you tackle as you travel throughout the canal system the more confident you will become. As I mentioned earlier you will usually find that, depending on the canal you are cruising on at the time, all the locks in the vicinity will be of the same design and type and operate in the same manner. Their individual maintenance, however, may not be so uniformly appreciated. You will come across some locks that will almost defy description. They will be hard to work and will take a couple of the crew to operate – at least! You'll remember them and will probably make a note of them in your cruising log with a few choice epithets!

One waterway which has very different methods of lock operating from the others is the River Nene in Northamptonshire, linking the Northampton arm of the Grand Union Canal with the Middle Level. These locks are known as guillotine locks and require considerable handling skill as you actually wind the lock gate up and the boat passes underneath. The number of turns required is high and some have a mind of their own.

Once again always refer to your cruising guide. That will forewarn you of all the locks you are going to meet and what type they are. There are now a large number of hydraulically operated locks on the system which are easier to manage, but it is the traditional forms of lock that you have

Looping the stern rope round a mooring post in a lock ...

... may mean the bow swings free as the water enters the chamber.

to work in the time-honoured and traditional fashion that will endear locks to you and make you appreciate what wonderful structures they are.

How to work locks going uphill – an illustrated guide

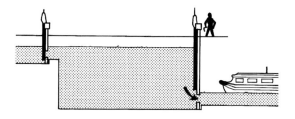

1. First make sure there aren't any boats coming the other way and wanting to go down. Check that the paddles at the top end are closed – then raise the paddles on the bottom gate.

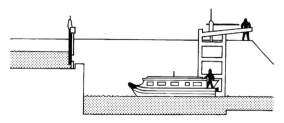

2. The water will escape through the paddles and the lock will empty. When the lock is empty you can open the gates and take the boat in. Before you close the gates, make sure no one else is coming – you should always wait and share locks. Remember to close the bottom paddles!

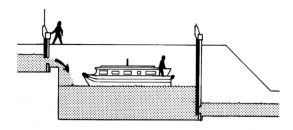

3. Now you can go to the top end of the lock and raise the top paddles. The water will come in and fill the lock – and the boat will rise to the top level.

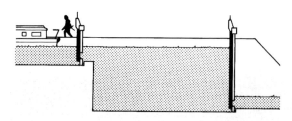

4. When the water is level on both sides of the top gates you can open them and go out. Before you leave the lock, check that all gates and paddles are closed – and that you've picked up your windlass and crew!

— 7 —
Safety for All

The knowledge a canal boater accrues over the years, or even over just a short period of time, can increase confidence every time he goes out on the water. Experience of locks, bridges, aqueducts and basic cruising common sense are obviously important for the future, as with any aspect of life, and the more you can appreciate the workings of each feature of the canal, the more you will enjoy your boating.

However, that enjoyment will always contain a nagging doubt if you are not sure whether you are doing things safely and in the correct manner. Safety on the water is imperative – not only for you and your crew but also for other boaters and the boat itself. Initially, you might think this is blatantly obvious but it's amazing how, on occasion, something is staring you straight in the face and you cannot see it. That is, until that something turns out to be disastrous.

Accidents will always happen of course, but it is to be fervently hoped not to you! Here, therefore, are what I believe to be important guidelines to steer you through some potential hazards when cruising on the canal and river system. I stress the word potential because what may be perceived to be a hazard by some will be totally ignored by others, boating on blissfully unaware. Safety on the water can be divided into a number of categories.

On the Canal

As I've mentioned earlier, the inland waterways system is exceptionally variable: broad or narrow canals, lots of locks or none at all, umpteen bridges, tunnels galore – what you come across will very

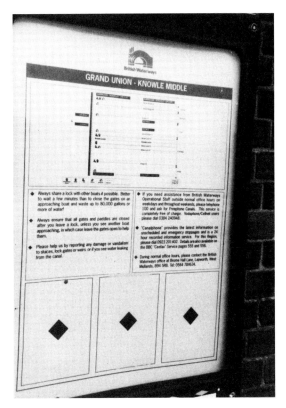

Read carefully any instructions for operating locks or equipment. They are normally displayed close by.

much depend on the route you have chosen. The way you approach any of these will reflect how much you have learned from your previous experiences. If you approach the obstacle in a sensible and straightforward way you will have nothing to worry about. If you are confident in what you know and in your ability then you are half-way there. However, you might not be equally confident in the abilities of the other folk on your boat. Both youngsters and older people need to be watched, and some mention of how they should be acting on the water might well be necessary.

Children should never play around on the boat when it is in motion. You might only be travelling at 4 miles per hour but water, at whatever speed, is not the natural element of human beings. Keep off the roof, no matter how tempting a leisurely sunbathe might be, until you are moored up, lest any slight movement dislodges you. This applies to all age groups. The fact that in many cases you are cruising through rural countryside often means overhanging branches from waterside trees drape over the canal itself. A hefty thwack from such a branch and the possibility of being swept into the water are best not experienced.

It's lovely sitting in the bow well, far away from the sound of the engine, enjoying the gentle swish of the boat gliding across the water. It might also seem lovely to sit on the gunwale dangling your feet in the cool water. This is actually one of the most potentially dangerous things you can do. The possibility of crushing your legs against the canal bank, a lock wall or bridge does not bear thinking about. Canal and river water is best appreciated from the boat itself and not by getting physically involved with it. The same applies when the boat is moored up. Bathing in the canal is also full of

hazard, as there is the risk of dangerous undercurrents which may not be apparent from the surface, and the chance of contacting Weils Disease (a potentially fatal infection from canal water polluted by rat's urine); it is definitely not worth it.

Canal boating is fun and, on occasion, exciting. Excitable folk tend to rush about and boats are no place for that. Excitement in a lock, tunnel or on an aqueduct can mean slipping off the boat and falling into the water, something you will most certainly want to avoid. Taking things easy and carefully and concentrating on what you are doing will keep you out of the canal or river. It might take you fractionally longer to achieve your goal than if you rush but you'll get there in the end without showing up either yourself or your crew.

If you do happen to fall into the water the best thing you can do is actually to stand up! Most canals are on average only three or four feet deep and towards the side this is often considerably less. Naturally, it's not going to be very pleasant as you are probably going to be standing in a lot of silty mud, but at least you will not have your head under the water. The most important thing to remember is not to panic.

On the Boat

As far as the boat on which you are cruising is concerned it is up to you to be fully familiar with its workings, and aware of any potential hazards that might occur if you have not taken the right precautions.

Just as in your own home on terra firma – if you don't live full time on the water, that is – you try to ensure that wherever a risk element is involved you know how to deal with it if things happen to go wrong. Outside on deck is the place

Definitely not the way to do it! Keep clear of the paddle and don't stand on the beam.

where, if an accident is going to occur, you are most likely to have a close encounter of the watery kind.

Slipping Off

Any water on the walking surfaces of the boat is going to make those surfaces slippery. The areas on a steel narrow boat that are going to be most prone to getting wet are the deck areas at the bow and stern and the gunwale running around the edge of the boat. Preventative measures can be taken with regard to both the boat and yourself.

Firstly, making sure those surfaces have some form of grip is very important. This can be created by adding sand or grit to the paint when it is applied. This will bulk out the paint and create the sort of finish that will give you confidence underfoot. Those areas indicated earlier would seem to be the ones most likely to need such treatment, but you should soon ascertain where on the boat you walk the most. Don't forget the cabin roof either. You never know when you need to take a short cut across that part and a non-slip finish is extremely necessary.

You can further enhance the effect of the non-slip finish by wearing deck shoes with a good tread. Always wear rubber-soled shoes on board, and not necessarily those with the really deep tread either. You will often find that shoes of that type tend to pick up a lot of dirt from the towpath and elsewhere, and more likely than not this is going to be taken onto the boat and be traipsed inside on the carpeting. If you want to maintain your popularity wear deck shoes or sensible trainers which will make you feel safe when the deck is wet. You will soon be able to judge their performance. The same applies to rubber boots or wellingtons. There are many types now available on the market and they have all been made with wet surfaces in mind. They also come in a variety of colours but that, of course, does not alter their effectiveness!

GRP boats tend to be more adversely affected by wet weather than steel ones. Surfaces can be even more slippery and on this occasion non-slip paint can't come to the rescue. However, there are additional surfaces that can be used. Plastic-ribbed tiling, which can be measured and cut to requirement, is excellent on both steel and glass-fibre boats.

It is also a good idea to attach a metal plate with a ribbed finish to that part of the gunwale that is used most frequently when entering or leaving the boat. It need only be nine inches or so in length and three inches wide (about 24 by 8cm) but it could well prove invaluable.

The other obvious piece of advice to prevent you from ending up in the water is to make sure you are holding on when you are doing any jobs around the boat. Make full use of the grab rails, wherever they are located, wherever you are on the boat. The general maxim of 'one hand for the boat and the other hand for yourself' is always worth remembering.

There are certain jobs which will need to be done from time to time which will necessitate full manoeuvrability around your craft – sweeping and mopping the decks down is one of the most obvious examples. Make sure that wherever you happen to be working at the time you are not leaving yourself in an unsupportable position where you could overbalance.

If you're not certain about distances between you and the canal bank don't take risks. Jumping off the boat is fine when you combine it with confidence. If there is the slightest chance of not making it, don't gamble. You're not being clever if you think you're saving time and then come a cropper!

Waterproofs, good waterproof boots and a life-jacket are part of canal gear to ensure safety, especially for youngsters.

Norfolk Broad cruising, with safety accentuated with the wearing of a life jacket.

Life Jackets and Life Buoys

For those members of the crew who are particularly unsure of themselves when moving about on the boat, and those who you feel unsure about, it's always worth insisting on the wearing of life jackets. Children may not be keen initially and might feel themselves to be too encumbered, but if you wear one yourself, and they are so brightly coloured these days, you should be able to convince them that it is 'cool' to wear one. Of course your confidence in all these matters will be considerably helped if you know that your crew can swim, but this need not be a prerequisite.

An essential part of any on-deck equipment is the life buoy, normally located towards the stern within easy reach of the person steering to be thrown to the victim in the water. You might like to consider having another one located towards the bow, either laid on the roof or hanging from a clip attached to a safety rail. Make sure everyone knows where they are.

Inside the Boat

When it comes to the interior of the boat, most safety aspects are connected with the risk of fire and the means of preventing or controlling it. The area where there is likely to be most risk of fire, if any, is the galley and in particular the cooker and its dependence on Calor gas. This is the most commonly used fuel, and if it is used safely it should present no problems whatsoever.

There are two or three things that need to be done if you are going to have peace of mind as far as the use of gas is concerned. If possible, install a gas alarm which will detect via a sensor any leak or inadvertent escape of gas. Whenever possible, install it in the lowest part of the boat, that is, the bilge. Gas is heavier than air and will always sink to the lowest point long before you are aware of its presence by smelling it.

Have a fire extinguisher nearby on the wall within easy reach of the cooker, and also a fire blanket to smother any flames igniting from over-heated cooking oil or chip fat. Again the accessibility of these will give you peace of mind, as you will feel prepared for any eventuality.

The other area of the boat where there is a potential fire risk is within the engine compartment, especially on boats with petrol engines. Installing bilge blowers to clear any possible build-up of fumes is a measure worth considering; use them before starting up the engine. When you are filling up with fuel make sure that any naked flames are extinguished to remove any possible risk of ignition.

You cannot afford to be negligent when it comes to safety on board. If you are, you are not just putting yourself at risk but the rest of your crew as well. Make sure that the other folk on board are aware of all the factors relating to their safety, and that they know what to do if some emergency does arise. With luck, fire extinguishers, gas alarms and lifebuoys will never be needed during your cruise and you will enjoy your time on the water without accident. However, it's always better to be wise before the event, and bearing in mind all the possibilities is always a sensible precaution.

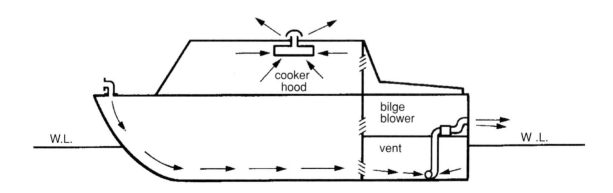

The cooker hood removes hot humid air; the bilge blower removes cold air, gas and petrol vapour.

— 8 —
The Crew

A collection of narrow boats in pleasant surroundings. A scene every boat owner hopes to appreciate.

In the long run, the success of your canal boating holiday and how much you enjoy it is going to depend very much on the rest of your crew. The crew, of course, can not only vary considerably in number – according to the size of your boat – but also in the members' ability to contribute to the journey as a whole. This ability to contribute will be directly affected by age and ability.

What is so exciting about canal and river holidays and cruising along at just 4 miles per hour is that it is entirely up to you where you go, what you see and how you do it. Whether you travel with friends

or family, however, you will need to be prepared to make allowances for individual needs which can vary considerably from person to person.

Children

Babies and Toddlers

Parents of very young children are often, understandably, somewhat dubious about taking them on canal boating holidays. After all, they are pretty much a handful on land, even before considering the additional problems that being on the water might create. Even so, when they are still at the carry-cot stage babies do make ideal passengers. Of course, you'll need to know the whereabouts of the launderettes en route and/or take a plentiful supply of disposable nappies and an equally plentiful supply of plastic bags to keep the soiled ones in until a convenient disposal point is reached.

If you overcome these relatively minor hiccups then taking baby with you is no problem at all. It is when the crawling stage has been reached that further measures have to be taken. When the carry-cot is outgrown but while bunk beds without sides are unsuitable because the children are still too small is an in-between stage that can prove restrictive. You can, however, buy bed guards which slot under the mattress and provide an 18in (46cm) high guard at the side of the bed.

Hire boat companies will often provide cot or bunk facilities with suitable guards. It's worth checking up on prior to booking if you're taking very young children along. It may be necessary to confine youngsters within a relatively small space by fitting gangway gates at the front or rear of the boat; hiring a television could also prove to be a boon. The enjoyment of watching their favourite programmes will be heightened by their being in really novel surroundings, and while you as a parent might think it's just great to get away from the 'box' on holiday, youngsters are certainly not going to appreciate this attitude!

It is your decision, of course, whether to take very young children with you or not, but as long as you take the right precautions you should be all right. Fit them with little life jackets if they have reached the toddling stage.

A good and inexpensive safety aid for toddlers is to clip their pram harness to a dog lead, which is then fastened to a suitable anchorage point. I know a boater who favours this method and perches his children on the cabin top to watch the world go by. Such dog leads are long enough to give young children some freedom of movement, like climbing up on a seat on deck, but not long enough to let them dangle over the side. In this context, it might be worth remembering that if you are hiring your boat, one with a deep bow well has advantages over one with a slightly dropped deck, as in these it will be harder for adventurous youngsters to reach the water.

Older Children

When children are somewhat older it is, initially, a great novelty to go on a boating holiday. Everything will be new and different and they will be very keen to give you a helping hand with simple little jobs around the boat. Make sure these little jobs are actually in the boat so you can keep an eye on them.

If you wear a life jacket yourself it should not prove too much of a problem to persuade children to wear one as well. Hire boat companies are very keen to have children go along and there will be jackets of all sizes available to suit everyone on board.

After two or three days, however, the novelty effect of boating will have begun to wear a bit thin and it is important to keep them occupied and above all, interested. You might still get the occasional, 'I'm bored!' remark but these will be easier to deal with if you give thought to what you can do to keep them amused before you even start your cruise. Children normally like the idea of a canal holiday and if they haven't been on one before, especially if they are a bit older, prepare them

It's a great adventure. These children have probably never cruised on a canal before.

for the fact that the cruise will be exciting, and, even if they are with their parents, it can be great fun as well. If your youngsters don't know very much about inland waterways buy a couple of interesting books on the subject. Most will have a little about the history of canals, the different boats you will see, wildlife, flowers and plants and usually also quite a bit about the canal features themselves – locks and how they work, tunnels, bridges and aqueducts.

Your holiday journey will pass through villages and towns, many with architectural features of note and interesting structures, stately homes and ancient churches. There is definitely no better way to absorb history than by cruising along on what was, for many years, our most important transport system.

I think it is essential to keep a log of your journey and youngsters love to get involved with the compilation of this. It could be a record to be enjoyed on many occasions throughout the years to come. Into it can go all kinds of interesting titbits, from the boat's name and a drawing of the layout, to the crew, details of the waterway structures and the times of passing them. Even the weather conditions can be noted, along with the names and types of other boats seen, and perhaps interesting names of pubs and why they are so named, and so on.

Drawings can form an important part of the log and if sufficient time is not available a quick sketch can be finished off later. In fact, when there are a number of children taking part it may even be necessary to provide extra books.

The youngsters on board will soon appreciate that the operation of the boat must be done with as much expertise as possible, so they will all be keen to learn the correct way of doing things. No scraping, no knocking and no banging of the boat is allowed! The crew must realize that you are the skipper and that every member of the family is a member of the crew. The safe working of the boat must come first, along with the safety of the individual. This will particularly apply at locks.

Make sure you inform the children that everybody, including them, must help in the running of the vessel. Involvement is the name of the game and the secret of satisfaction for all the crew. Both girls and boys can steer, so all can learn – with the comforting advice that some take longer than others to get the feel of the boat and to develop confidence in their ability.

It is up to the skipper to decide when a crew member is capable of being left alone to cope. A few distinct, pre-arranged hand signals will give a young helmsman even more confidence when going solo. Actions will thus be confirmed by the skipper at a glance. Shouting will only confuse and can create a bad session of nerves, long faces and tears.

Along with steering and handling of the boat go the important points of sound signals and the handling of ropes. Youngsters, after a little practice beforehand with a clothes line, can then coil, throw or tie ropes, skills that are an asset when mooring. Other duties dealing with the boat itself, such as swabbing the decks, filling the water tanks and so on, should be done on a rota basis so that everyone gets a fair share of the fun.

Galley duties should also be shared and there are no excuses. The adults want a rest too! If Mum usually does all the cooking, for example, it's not a bad idea to have a 'Mum's day off' from the galley duties, which can involve the whole crew in having a glorious day, finishing off with an evening meal made by the children. That can be great for all concerned. Try it! Meanwhile, Mum could

A party of youngsters well kitted out for a cruise.

start her day by checking the engine oil, followed by a turn at the helm as well as lock and swing bridge duties. It would be great fun for her, too! She would soon realize that it's no wonder that the children always clean their plates so quickly!

Each day will pass by with so much to do. With the boat travelling at walking pace, members of the crew can hop off at a bridge hole to go for a short nature ramble on the towpath. There will be plenty to see. So, really, all a child needs to take along to enjoy a holiday is a notebook, a drawing book, a book for the log, plenty of pencils, a cruising guide and a book on canals, plus, perhaps, a pack of cards

Giving a hand when necessary. Young ones love it but of course they need to be watched.

and a boxed game for wet evenings.

There are a few basic rules for all members of the crew of which youngsters should be fully aware:

1. No running around the locks; walk on all occasions.
2. Take care when operating locks.
3. Always put the safety catch on paddle gear.
4. Use the boat as if it were your very own.
5. Never jump either onto or off the boat unless you are sure you can land safely.
6. Remember, everyone else on board is a member of the crew, not just you especially. It's a joint effort, and everyone helps one another.

Mopping down the decks is an integral part of the crew's duties – but only when the boat is securely moored.

You will probably find that sometimes one good youngster is a better crewman than six adults! If you follow the above guidelines, having the children aboard will make your holiday so much more fascinating and fun both for you and them.

Older Crew Members

Taking elderly folk with you on your holiday should also not present you with any problems. Unlike children, grandparents will need less in the way of physical activity to keep them occupied and more in the way of good vantage points from where they can see what's going on. Boats with good all-round visibility, deep windows and a raised seating or dining area will be a tremendous advantage. The cruiser style of narrow boat with a large bow well and rear deck will mean that they can be out where the action is. They may not actually be able to help in the workings and day-to-day running of the boat so much, but they will have a lot of suggestions to make and advice to offer.

They will enjoy the slower pace of life that is experienced during a boating holiday and they will also enjoy the occasional stop-offs to visit interesting places en route. If you plan your journey around some fascinating waterway structures that you know the older ones will like, they will feel very much involved as well.

If you are taking elderly and possibly infirm crew with you there are lots of ways to keep them happy and amused. How about 'theme days' where all the crew can participate in dressing up according to the theme and serving up meals and snacks that complement the theme as well. They can be tremendous fun as you can all create your own little world away from everybody else. Nobody else need know but keeping a record in

photographs will bring back many happy holiday memories again later.

You may have handicapped crew members on board – whether physically or mentally. Again, this need not be a daunting prospect at all. If you want to take a physically handicapped person with you on holiday all you have to do beforehand is check that the hire company with which you are intending to book your boat can provide one that can specifically cater for such needs. A wheelchair can easily be fitted on board if there is a wide and broad rear or bow deck, wider exits and entrances as well as a gangway which is just that little bit more accommodating. There are many companies now whose hire fleets contain narrow boats that have been purpose-built and fitted out for handicapped requirements. Remember that these requirements also include the toilet/washing facilities that are so important for us all. Ease of access in and out and also of straightforward manoeuvrability can be achieved to such an extent that by incorporating slightly raised platforms a wheelchair-bound member of the crew can actually steer the boat.

The involvement of the mentally handicapped in canal boating is now greater than it has ever been before. No matter what their age, the look of wonder to be seen on handicapped people's faces as they experience boating, possibly for the first time, is really fantastic to see. Combining this with some form of music on board and then maybe an inland waterways holiday, will be a heart-warming experience. There are many specialist groups that organize boating trips and holidays, whether a short break or not, for the mentally and physically handicapped and you can rest assured that they will be wonderfully looked after by trained professional staff.

I don't think there is any other form of

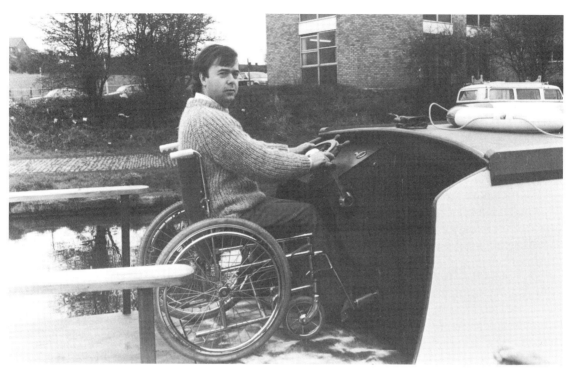

Taking control from the stern for this spinally injured boater.

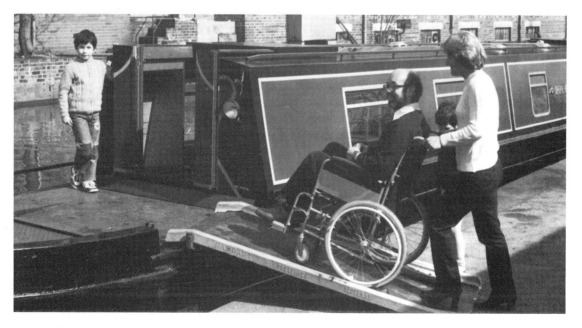

A ramp leading up onto the rear deck gives easy access for wheelchairs.

holiday enjoyment that can be so universally appreciated – by all age groups of whatever physical or mental ability – as a canal boating holiday. The very fact that such holidays are so adaptable and can meet a wide variety of needs makes them enormously attractive. Being aware of how to tailor the holiday to suit your own party's needs can snuff out any nagging doubts about suitability and can help ensure everyone's satisfaction.

— 9 —

Boating on Your Own

After all you have read so far you could well be excused for thinking that if you have not yet fully grasped the canal boating situation any limitation of crew members to help you would be regarded as silly. You would be perfectly correct to feel like that; any change in your circumstances would be your decision entirely.

You are not likely even to contemplate boating on your own until you have mastered the rudiments and become experienced in coping with all that goes with canal cruising. However, this statement of the obvious doesn't necessarily mean you will never have to know what to do in every situation because you will always have someone with you. Solo boating may be thrust upon you unexpectedly but as far as this chapter is concerned I am assuming that the choice to do so is totally yours. You are still going to plan your journey fully before you set off, but on this occasion you should bear in mind that you will have to be prepared to adapt methods and make short cuts so that your journey can be accomplished alone.

Your Boat and You

As soon as you know what sort of boat you are going to be cruising on, you need to look at it carefully to judge where you can benefit from any helping hands that will make life easier for you. The length of the boat will be very important. The longer it is the more difficult it will be to cope; it won't be impossible but it will be very much harder. The length of the boat, and whether it is a narrow boat or an inland cruiser, will seriously affect the task ahead of you. As I have mentioned earlier, the ropes that stabilize your craft and from where you can assert as much influence as possible from the land, are attached at the bow and stern ends. An additional rope, attached centrally on either side, will be a great help when pulling the boat into the bank and will ensure better handling and mooring up.

The tiller arm can also be adapted to make it easier to steer and deal with other matters as well. I remember going on a long-distance cruise on the Lancaster Canal some years ago on a semi-traditional boat which had just such an adaptation to the tiller arm. This took the form of an extension that took the tiller arm into the boat so that you were protected from the weather but could still progress. Of course, to move the tiller left or right now required much greater movement of the arm, but the piping extension that was slotted over the end of the tiller made steering very easy indeed.

Access onto, round and over your boat will need to be as easy as possible. You will on occasion be in situations where you will have to be able to move about the boat as quickly as possible; efficient mastery will enable you to tackle any problems that arise. A small step attached to the cabin side towards the stern and one towards the bow will make it much easier

Going for it! A solo boater on a traditional narrow boat.

to get up onto the cabin roof. Forget about walking round the gunwale to get from stern to bow or vice-versa – walking on the cabin roof is a great short cut. There is all the more reason, therefore, to check that your non-slip measures on board are adequate, as discussed in Chapter 7.

Be Prepared

Before you set off everything should be ready on deck. It's a good idea to have a long line with the ends attached to each end of the boat stored together with the boat hook and boat pole on the roof. Check your map very carefully and plan where you intend to go each day. It's not worth travelling for mile after mile only to find as it begins to get dark that you are either in the middle of nowhere or in the middle of a long and laborious flight of locks. Your map or guidebook will also tell you which side of the canal the towpath is located and this should help you sort your ropes in the most effective way.

You will find your windlass is one of the most important pieces of equipment on board. If possible, wear a good strong belt in which to tuck it, or a stout jacket under which you can carry the windlass over your shoulder. Using either of these methods will ensure that you can keep both your hands free at all times.

Just prior to setting off, coil your ropes so that they are within easy reach of your steering position. Doing this should prevent those few moments of undue delay when you are intending to moor up but the boat begins to drift a bit away from the bank while you look for the ropes! Have a single rope attached to the stern with an eye splice that is big enough to slip onto a bollard or cleat at whichever side of the boat is required. Give it a round turn as well, which should prevent it from slipping off.

Locks

Lock-operating principles remain the same whether you are part of a crew or on your own. What does change is who does the individual tasks – that person is always going to be you so you will need to have a plan of action. You will normally be able to see if someone is already working the lock. If there is, it might be worth while going ashore to make sure that they don't close the lock in your face, or even leave it open at the other end.

Some boaters you will meet like to get as close to the gates themselves as possible. In fact some even push the gates open with the boat itself. I certainly would not recommend this for the simple reason that you can never completely judge the time or the moment to do this and you could well end up damaging the gate. However, if you can judge where to stop the boat to within an inch or two of the gate, and none of the possible snags to prevent you continuing with the lock operation are present and everything is in your favour, then it does save time, when you are solo boating.

Some boaters suggest that they can cope perfectly well by keeping the boat as near as possible to the actual workings, but you need to make sure you have suitable fenders fitted before you try this. Also never force the workings by pushing against the gates, as this can strain them unduly and eventually cause them to leak. If you have to moor up before opening the lock gates, try to get as close as you can without actually causing an obstruction. Tie up fairly loosely and leave the engine running.

Going Up

If you have to empty the lock, open the first paddle really slowly so there is not a

It's far easier for a solo boater to operate the single gate of a narrow lock.

tremendous rush of water that could push your boat out of the way. It would then be out of reach or may even be drawn back towards the gates as a back eddy develops. When the lock is emptied, lean against the balance beam to open the gate as soon as the levels are equal. Then pull the boat through the lock – slowly – by the tow rope; you will find that there is ample time to lower the paddle and the gate before you get back on board, via the cabin roof.

Remember never to let the boat run ahead under its own steam within the lock, as hitting the top gate or cill could damage both. Resting the bow of the boat against the top gate is also not recom-

mended as the forward well of the boat could become flooded, either from leaks in the gates or when the paddles are being opened. In addition a boat rising in the water could be caught under gate projections, fill with water and sink.

After the gate is closed behind you, you can open the top gate paddles, ground paddles first. You will soon be able to judge the speed at which to do this most successfully. The boat will always run back towards the bottom gates and will often touch them, but after a short while, as the water within the lock begins to circulate, it will begin to move forwards again. If it looks as if the bow will hit the top gate it is only a short step onto the

An inland cruiser in a wide lock, holding the boat in with the boat hook.

Mooring bollard, access steps, foot grips near the lock beam. Make use of what's there.

boat to put the engine in reverse again to halt this movement.

When the lock is nearly full this water current effect will have practically ceased, at which time, when the levels are equal either side, you can nip back on board and gradually take your boat through until the stern is out. Then hold her back with slight reverse, which should keep her just about stationary long enough to close the paddles and gates behind you. This usually works with a steel boat but with a lighter cruiser you will need to take a rope ashore with you in case she begins to drift away. You don't necessarily have to tie it to

anything really but having it with you gives you that bit more confidence.

When you are in a wide lock never leave your boat floating about without being tied to the side. If you do, it will ricochet from side to side – sometimes quite violently as the water catches it. It is best to tie the bow back to the centre bollard and maybe even secure the stern to the same one. When filling the lock, open the ground paddle on the same side as the boat. This means that the water coming into the lock will bounce off the opposite wall onto the side of the boat and consequently hold it into the side. You only need to open the other ground paddle about half-way. You can then go to the gate paddles in the same order as before.

Open and close the paddle in the normal way, and if you are entering the lock when it is empty you can take full advantage of the lock ladders at the side of the lock chambers.

Under these circumstances you will gain considerable height by standing on the cabin roof so you won't have to wait until the boat has fully risen with the water level before you are able to hop off. Make sure you have the necessary ropes to hand and with the boat hook catch the lock ladder to haul the boat into the side and keep it there. In addition, take advantage of any help that might be to hand, especially in a breasted-up situation with another boat. If you have other folk working through the same lock let them take some responsibility and do their full share! They will soon come to realize that their help will be very much appreciated by you. Use the ropes you have attached at either end of the boat as effectively as you can. By standing centrally on the cabin roof with each rope looped over the bollard you will have full control of the boat while it is in the lock moving up (or down) with the water.

Going Down

The approach to the lock is just the same as when going up, except this time the bow of the boat will be higher than the gate so make sure you don't touch the handrail or the paddle gear. Frequently it is pretty difficult to keep the boat straight, so don't leave it in gear unless you have a stern rope out onto the towpath. Then open the gate and steer the boat in. Never let the boat force its way in, as damage to the lock, and your boat, can occur.

If you are in a deep lock take the long rope ashore and loop it over the centre bollard in case you can't get back on board. Don't tie it. As the water goes down watch it all the while and gradually ease out the rope.

In narrow locks a boat left unattended will drift down towards the bottom gates, so check with the line or use reverse to prevent the boat hitting them. When the water is at equal levels, open the gates and shut the paddles. You can then drive, or pull if necessary, the boat out of the lock. Stop, once again, at the entrance to give you the opportunity to close the gates and the paddles. On small locks you may even be able to pull the gate shut by hand as you go slowly through!

If, as occasionally happens, you find your boat out of reach at the bottom of a deep lock, you can actually 'flush' it out by opening one head paddle a little bit and then closing it when the boat is half-way through the bottom gates. You can then get back on board and stop the boat by using the engine.

It's Not Easy

It is certainly not easy boating on your own and you are bound to come across the occasional problem that you have not foreseen and that will take a bit of thinking out. Only really contemplate going it alone when you have built up your confidence through boating with others as part of your crew. You will soon be able to suss out little tricks that will help you in certain circumstances when on your own.

Swing and lift bridges often have all their important working parts on the opposite side of the canal to the towpath. You will then have to nudge your boat over to that side before you get off to do the necessaries. Make sure the boat is tied up well so that she doesn't drift off. Sometimes you will find yourself disembarking into the unknown when your footing may not be on as firm a ground as you would wish. Similarly, the ground may be considerably obscured by copious amounts of undergrowth, sometimes waist high. You might well be smiling and nodding in sympathy as you read this, but for the most part it all adds to the fun of boating.

Boating alone requires extra care, but the experience you gain will be certainly immeasurable and rewarding.

— 10 —
Overcoming Any Problems

To suggest that there might be some problems during your cruise would, on the face of it, seem to be a somewhat negative stand-point. 'Accentuating the positive', as the song goes, is all very well, but if you are unable to appreciate that things can go wrong from time to time you would be living under a false premiss.

The following guidelines indicate the possible problems that could occur. Hopefully they won't, but if you know what to do when a problem arises then it will probably give you much more confidence in tackling it.

Problems on the Canal

Too Much Water

Strong currents and even flooding, for the most part, are generally a problem only on rivers and usually in winter – though not always. After a period of heavy rain a close watch on the weather conditions will give you a good indication of what you are likely to encounter if you are going river boating. Some canal navigations also merge with rivers for part of their length and can therefore be subject to the same problems as rivers, and it's worth knowing if you are going to be affected.

Before you venture out onto a river with fast-flowing water you need to be very sure that your boat can actually cope with such conditions, against the current, so having the correct engine to give

you sufficient power is imperative. River boating is very different from canal boating (as you will see in Chapter 11). Water flows faster where the river narrows and also under bridges, so you need to be certain that you can cope with these potential obstacles as well and that you can stop when necessary.

If the river meanders, and they all do, remember that the current will be more noticeable on the outside of the bend, while on the inside it will be less strong and the water shallower. This is because silt is deposited on the inside of bends. So if you are going against the current keep to the inside but try to avoid running aground. Stick to the outside when cruising with the current. If the stretch of river you are on is relatively straight, keep to the middle as the strongest current will be found there.

Locks on rivers will normally be accompanied by weirs and it is vital you avoid these. There will be clear signs indicating where to go so keep well away from the weir stream. The current will be heading in that direction and certainly not towards the lock. Once again, sufficient engine power is all that's needed. On the Rivers Severn, Avon and Trent the weirs are of the over-fall type and may not be so easy to distinguish, so it's very important to keep an eye on your map or guide to the waterway so you know exactly when to expect them.

On the River Thames the weirs are normally of the sluice type and will not let a

A fast-flowing overflow channel exists beyond the lock. Be ready as the boat might get caught up in it and swing you over to the opposite side. Sufficient power from the engine, however, will overcome any difficulties.

large boat pass through them. Even so, the water can pass through with considerable force and there have been instances of boats being caught up against them in the past. Fortunately you don't have to rely totally on your own experience and intuition when it comes to boating on a fast-flowing river. The local water authority will have put up signs warning boaters of the state of the water in the river and whether levels will be too high to negotiate bridges. Keep a wary eye out for these warning signs. They are there for your own protection and safety,

and instructions on them must be strictly adhered to. Hire companies whose boats use river navigations will not allow their craft to move at all when conditions are dangerous, which is a very sensible decision. The private boat owner has to make that decision himself and would be advised to do likewise.

Even if the water in the river is at normal levels and everything appears to be straightforward, it is as well to remember that there are cross-currents and eddies which can alter the handling of your boat and consequently the manner in which

Rubbish collecting over this overflow should indicate to the boater where there is likely to be an increase in current.

you approach locks and bridges. On these occasions it is advisable not to go too slowly as a lack of power could mean you lose total control at a time when you need it most. If you go fairly steadily you can always put the boat briefly into reverse to slow down.

Running Aground

You can get stuck if the water levels are high and you cannot exactly define where the banks are on the river, so you may get caught up on tree stumps or even submerged pontoons. If there is a risk of this happening, it's best to tie up to a tree or other fixed point by using long lengths of rope both well astern and ahead of your boat. By doing this you should avoid the hang-up syndrome when the water level lowers. Also throw the anchor well ahead and out from the bank to keep the boat more secure.

If you are going to have to stay on board for a considerable length of time,

A drained waterway shows the shape of the cut and how shallow it is near the edge.

keep checking the condition of the river and the level of the water around and make the necessary adjustments. If you find you are becoming stranded as the water level lowers, get everybody on board onto the opposite side away from the point of contact, and use your engine to reverse away from that point. Moving the boat backwards and forwards or even with a see-saw effect should help you get off the obstruction while preventing you from driving yourself even harder aground.

If you still find yourself stuck, try to get other boaters to give you a helping hand by pushing or towing you off. In a real emergency the police, boatyards, the navigation authority or even farmers with tractors might well come to your rescue.

The completely opposite scenario to being stuck when there is too much water, is coming to a complete standstill when there is not enough water in the canal, either because dredging has been insufficient or for some other reason, so the bottom of the canal is far too near the top! This is the most infuriating stoppage to your progress. It seems so unnecessary on occasion, particularly when there appears to have been ample rainfall. Use of the boat pole combined with judicious use of the engine should enable you to effect a hasty release and ease the boat off the mud.

The entrance to a lock showing what it is like with water drained from the adjacent pound.

Bridges

As mentioned earlier, bridges are only as hazardous as you make them. Lining up the boat before making the final approach should ensure safe and smooth entrance and exit through the bridge hole; although the occasional 'bang and ricochet' effect cannot be avoided, with luck you will escape with only a slight graze to boat or bridge. The other hazard can be the height of the bridge – if it's too low or your boat is too high.

To get round this problem, as you approach the bridge stand with your eyes level with the highest point of the boat. You should then be able to judge whether you will fit underneath, although it's by no means easy. If you can see the arch of the bridge on the far side you should be able to get through. Remember to lower any chimneys, aerials and other protrusions. If you are on a river and heading with the flow downstream, and you don't

Use the space available with forward and reverse when necessary.

A tight fit, so heads down when passing under a low bridge.

think you'll get under a bridge, turn round as quickly as possible rather than trying to use reverse, which won't normally be powerful enough. If you do get stuck you will basically be dependent on help from others. If they know what they are doing you will be in safe hands but check that they are insured first – you don't really want to have to state on any claim form that you only incurred damage to your boat when somebody else got involved in helping you out!

Problems on the Boat

Engine Trouble

Your engine packing up can be the most frustrating problem of the lot. You feel totally helpless when your engine suddenly dies – if you have no idea what the problem is you are in a really awkward predicament. On a canal you should normally be able to get over to the side, tie up and check out the situation. Contacting the hire company or a nearby boatyard should be pretty straightforward but might require a fairly long hike to the nearest phone box. You have to be patient in any case as it might be a while before you can be rescued.

When the engine packs up on a fairly wide river and you are at the mercy of the flow, it's a slightly different matter. People are bound to wonder what on earth you are doing swinging about in the river – your red face will only add to their *joie de vivre*. Four blasts of your hooter – meaning 'I am unable to manoeuvre' – may attract the right sort of attention. Otherwise use the anchor. It is there for such emergencies so don't forget you have it. The anchor rope should be marked in feet or metres to give you some indication of depth. Don't drop the anchor where you may run over it, and pay out enough rope so that it will bite and not drag along.

There's Something Around the Prop!

When you don't seem to be making any progress whatsoever, there's a lack of response from the engine and it begins to overheat or even emit black smoke, more likely than not the prop will be the root of the problem. On a narrow boat with a weed hatch this is easily sorted out. Tie up, switch off the engine, take out the key and only then remove the weed hatch. Roll your sleeve up to your armpit and have a good feel down amongst the centre of things. I'm always a bit wary about this grope into the unknown but the offending detritus is usually perfectly innocuous and can be easily disentangled from the propeller and propeller shaft. Wire or the occasional mattress spring will take a little longer: use cutters or a good strong pair of pliers to free the prop. You can now buy a cutter that is fitted adjacent to the prop and will automatically cut through anything that causes a problem. It might be worth fitting one of those. Of course the area the canal passes through may well determine the underwater possibilities – for example, there is more likely to be junk in the canal in an urban area. This should help you ascertain whether there is a likelihood of your prop snaring or not.

You don't always have to resort to removing the weed hatch. If the obstruction is just a plastic bag or a conglomeration of weed, a few sharp bursts forward and backwards should free your prop from the offending item. You might be able to fish it out with a boat hook and throw it to one side to make sure that it won't become tangled up with your prop again. When that happens it's time for a few choice words!

No matter what, always check the prop on a regular basis, especially if you have run aground or the *objet d'art* was particularly stubborn. A bent or damaged propeller can cause damage to the bearings and produce an unpleasant vibration throughout the whole boat.

In Tow

I mentioned earlier that you might have to be rescued from an awkward situation by being towed off. Of course it might be you who is actually doing the rescuing. In this case it's best to use a long tow rope and have the boat steered or towed alongside. If the said craft is without a rudder the side-by-side method will be far preferable. Basically, you need to lash the other boat to the side of your own, but take it as far back as you can to make it easier to steer. With ropes from bow to stern, bow to stern, stern to stern and bow to bow you will have accounted for all contingencies and variables. Secure in this knowledge and secure with your ropes, you will be able to tow successfully.

Fire

I dealt with what to do if fire breaks out on board in Chapter 7, but it does no harm to reiterate the advice here.

If an ignited fat fire breaks out in the galley, cover the fire with a damp cloth, not a wet one, as this will prevent any egress of oxygen. Never put water on the flaming fat or throw it into the canal as this will only cause the fat to splatter everywhere – amazingly so. Other fires in the galley may be caused by over-cooking something in the oven because you've forgotten it's there. When it comes to lighting the gas rings, the grill or the oven, if you are not completely *au fait* with how to do it, let someone perform that duty who

does know. Watch it being done and you will soon learn the knack.

Fire could also break out if there is an electrical fault or if the engine overheats. An unlagged exhaust pipe or a carelessly dropped lighted cigarette might also be sufficient to ignite a possible accumulation of gas or petrol vapour in the bilges. If you do happen to smell gas or petrol make sure you ventilate the boat well.

If you can see only smoke, always remember to identify and isolate the source as quickly as possible. Don't take any chances – turn off the oven, switch off the batteries, stop the engine, turn off the gas bottles and turn off the fuel.

If you see flames use a dry powder extinguisher to put them out. A couple of two-second blasts at the base of the flames should reduce their fervour. At the same time manoeuvre the boat away from other craft or buildings. Use buckets or pans of water, of which there's plenty about, if necessary. Get everyone who is not actually involved in fighting the fire off the boat. When the fire is out it must be reported to the navigation authority and the fire brigade. It is more than likely that one or both of these will need to make an inspection with a view to preventing future fires breaking out on other boats.

First Aid

One of the essential items of equipment on every boat is a good and comprehensive first-aid kit. Include plasters, a selection of bandages and standard dressings in addition to eye pads, slings and triangular bandages. The usual safety pins, cotton wool, disinfectant and creams for sunburn and mosquito bites are a must. Above all, make sure you have full instructions for their use.

If you have the opportunity to go on a St John Ambulance first-aid course, do so. The experience to be gained by so doing is invaluable, not only for you but to the rest of your crew as well.

With a bit of luck the majority of the 'problems' mentioned above will never occur on your boat or happen to your crew. However, the possibility that they might arise is worth bearing in mind so that contingency plans can swing into action straight away if they do, without wasting valuable time panicking. To be forewarned is to be forearmed.

— 11 —
River Cruising

Many boaters who have spent most of their time exploring the canal system with all its intricacies believe that if they have a boat designed, built or hired for that purpose it is to these areas that they should confine their cruising. True, the style of craft frequently dictates the style of boating and where any element comes in that could possibly alter this then it may be a case of being safe rather than sorry and sticking to what your boat is designed for.

Granted, canal boating is a skill in its own right but many parts of the inland waterways system do take in and merge with rivers and river navigations and the

Wide waters, small boat. Be prepared before you set off.

accompanying flow of water either because of direction or tidal influence. A narrow boat owner may understandably believe that the design of his boat with its truncated shape and flat bottom is not the right one for handling rivers, and therefore he will steer clear of a route that requires him to do so. However, this concern is usually unfounded if you have the know-how to handle your boat sensibly,

Warning signs give an indication of the state of the river. Read them carefully.

are aware of the situation at all times, and take it steady.

Always check that the engine on your boat is of sufficient power to cope with a current or a tide. The boat will only respond to available power and it would be foolhardy to think otherwise. On a river there are a number of additional outside influences that can affect, help or hinder your progress. Therefore make sure that you can benefit from the aspects that will improve your cruise on the one hand, but have the wherewithal to cope with those incidents that can cause you problems on the other. There are often warning signs which give an indication of the state of a river; always read them carefully.

Inland Cruisers

Whether you are standing by a lock on the River Thames or sitting in the beer garden of a Norfolk Broads pub watching the scene, you will not have failed to notice that GRP cruisers abound on these rivers. They far outnumber any other form of powered craft and are very much on a par with sailing boats. The first rule of the river is always to remember that when there is a mixture of boats on the water, power always give way to sail. This is a statement of the obvious, perhaps, but is sometimes forgotten when you see sailing boats tacking to and fro. GRP boats, naturally, are far lighter and far more easy to manoeuvre than their heavier steel counterparts. Their shape and hull design enhance this: a definite extension of the hull into the water will enable it to hold the water more firmly, while tapering off towards the bow will create more of a streamlining effect. Smooth passage through the water is essential if the boat is going to be handled with ease.

Steering

Steering, in the form of a steering wheel, is far more reminiscent of handling a car than a narrow boat with the left to right response, but that is where the similarity ends. The surface on which you are travelling is often moving, as are you, so you can go sideways, diagonally and backwards in quick succession and to cap it all you don't have any brakes to bring you to a stop! The stern of your boat can seem to have a mind of its own whilst the bow seems to be responding to all your requests from the wheel. How well your boat responds to your steering will depend on the system of steering or drive you have.

There are several different layouts available. The first form is the inland cruiser with an inboard engine which has its rudder in front of the propeller. The second is the cruiser with an outboard engine fixed to the transom. The third is known as the outdrive system, which, although it has the engine within the boat, has a steering extension which projects beyond the transom. Boats with the second and third forms of steering will handle similarly as it is the propeller that creates the power and direction, while the first form has a rudder that acts with the prop.

When you first switch on your engine make sure, before you do anything else, that the steering wheel responds easily and smoothly. Similarly, the actual controls should not be so stiff that you have to put in a good amount of effort in order to get anywhere. Straining your controls and steering wheel can prove disastrous in the long run: it is far better to check everything initially.

You will find that an inland cruiser with an inboard engine, a deeper keel and a rudder, has considerably more stability than boats powered with an outboard. The latter normally have a pretty shallow draught and not much of a keel. Therefore reactions to what you do will be quicker and more forceful if you don't remember to take it steady.

I know that I have found when changing from boat to boat and between different forms of steering that it can be a little unnerving at first and difficult to get the judgement absolutely right. The more solid response from an inboard engine is slower and therefore you react accordingly. An outboard engine on the transom not only has a different sound but also responds far more quickly to the slightest touch on the throttle, both in speed and direction. Sorting this out, if you have been used to another steering system, can take a little while so it might be worth practising a few basic manoeuvres with the system that you have before you actually get underway.

If your first experience of river boat handling is in a hire boat, then you will be given some form of instruction, both theoretical and practical. Similarly, if you buy a new boat you won't be allowed just to go off willy-nilly and discover everything for yourself. It's far more positive than that. The initial instruction that you will be given will teach you the rudiments of boat control and your ever-increasing experience will obviously add to this, but it is quite a steep learning curve.

Setting Off and Mooring Up

Setting Off

Whatever type of steering system you have on your boat, check, while it is still moored up, the directional effects that various movements on the wheel and pressure of river water on the bow end of

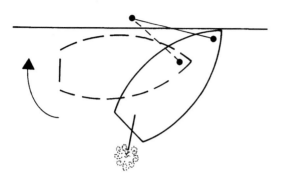

With an outboard engine, turning the wheel to the right will be the best way to turn the stern in.

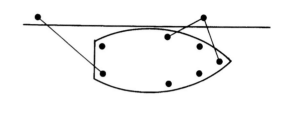

Tie ropes from bank to boat to prevent banging about on a flowing waterway.

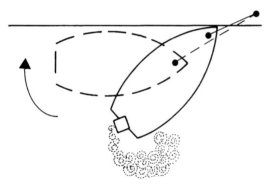

Use the wash created by the engine to bring the boat in from a fixed point at the bow end.

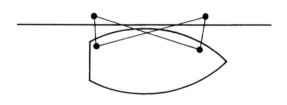

Ropes tied like this will provide maximum security when moored.

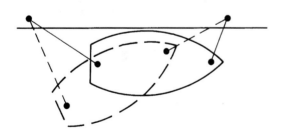

Once again, correct positioning of ropes will ease the boat in.

throttle will create. Look over the side at the water and see what it does, the force in which it is directed and how this can affect your handling of the boat. Turning left and right or just steering a straight course might, on the face of it, seem pretty straightforward but there are factors on the river other than just the steering on the boat that can influence the boat's response to your actions.

The flow of the water and the direction you are pointing in at the time can mean you have some difficulty getting away from your moorings in the first place. Constant pressure of water on the bow end of your boat will probably mean that you have to reverse out using the power of the engine to overcome the power of the water. It is far better to have prepared for this earlier when you initially moored up by have the boat facing into the flow of water, so that when you want to set off the current can help you by easing the boat round and consequently away from the moorings. This applies to both river and sea tidal flow where it exists.

Furthermore, it is worth remembering that the strength of the wind can also considerably affect the quality of your manoeuvring. A strong and steady wind blowing against the side of your boat can hold you against the bank with the draught acting as a sail. Careful use of the engine in both forward and reverse gears should get you away from your moorings, and take full advantage of the current or tide to help you as well. There's nothing quite so infuriating as finding yourself held back and in danger of colliding with other boats moored nearby.

The 'Paddlewheel' Effect

This is the term used to describe the effect the water being churned up by the propeller can have on the rudder, producing the opposite directional steering from that required by the wheel. Being aware of this effect is certainly worth while as you can use it both in mooring up and leaving. A burst of the throttle can bring the stern in quite dramatically, and quickly produce a really confident movement of the boat to start your mooring procedure.

Let the rest of your crew know what you intend to do when mooring up or setting off. They can be invaluable in helping you out and letting you know exactly what the situation is at the stern of the boat. If your steering position is amid-

ships you may not have good all-round visibility so extra pairs of eyes will be a great help. Inform your crew how much you are relying on them and they will feel that they are making a valuable contribution to the success of your cruise.

Underway

Once you are out on the river away from your mooring you will be able to concentrate on the more enjoyable prospect of steering the boat and at the same time

Floating pontoons on rivers affixed to substantial posts, which allow for the rise and fall of the water. This one is on the River Trent near the entrance to the Erewash Canal.

Moving off with twin screws

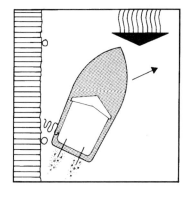 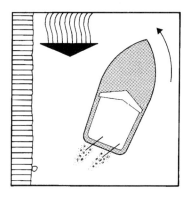 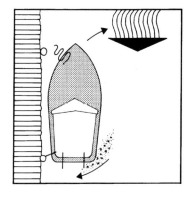

As the bow moves out, let go stern line and slow ahead port; slow ahead starboard.

When well clear of berth and other vessels increase power and start using the wheel.

Wheel amidships; let go forward; short burst of slow astern starboard.

Leaving an alongside berth when heading into the stream

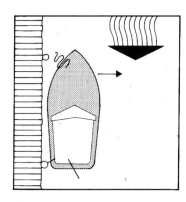 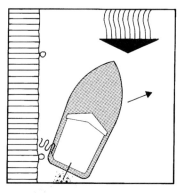 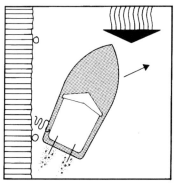

Engine in neutral; wheel to starboard; let go bow line.

As the current carries the bow out, wheel amidships; slow ahead; let go stern line.

Once clear of berth and other craft increase power.

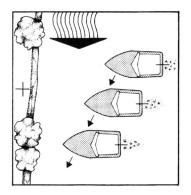

Going across the current the whole craft will be carried sideways.

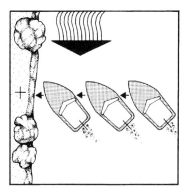

With a five knot current (which you should not encounter too often) and a boat speed of five knots you would need to head into the current at about 45 degrees to hold your line.

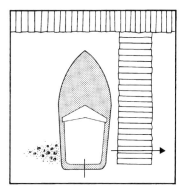

Checking the paddlewheel effect. With the engine going astern this boat will move to starboard. When going ahead the paddlewheel effect is much less evident.

making progress. The faster you go – although speed is frequently restricted on rivers, or your engine might be adjusted to prevent you from going too fast – the more quickly the boat will respond to the rudder. The more slowly you go the more you will have to turn the wheel to achieve the same response.

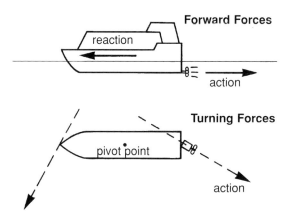

Your crew can also affect the movement of your boat and its stability in the water, particularly if your inland cruiser is a small one and the members of your crew are big. You will find that the boat will rock and move from side to side accordingly as they move about so try to restrict lots of to-ing and fro-ing on a small boat whilst under way. There won't be any problem on a larger cruiser but even so make sure you know where the crew are.

Stopping and Mooring Up

River boating can be just as absorbing as canal boating. Use your river map, guidebook or chart in the same way as a canal guide to plan ahead where you are going. There won't be so many opportunities to stop and moor up on the river, so you will need to check up where there are such places so that you can time your arrival

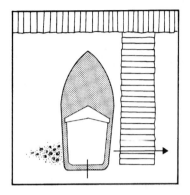 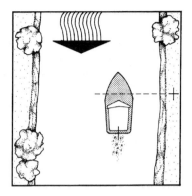 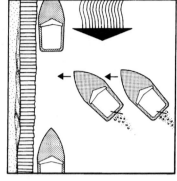

Always turn so that you can use the paddlewheel effect of the propeller to push your stern around, but remember that you must have the rudder in the correct position before engaging gear.

To make progress your speed through the water must exceed the speed of the current. By balancing your speed through the water against the speed of the current you should be able to hold your craft stationary.

By careful use of the throttle and rudder you can make your boat travel sideways or crab across the current into a berth.

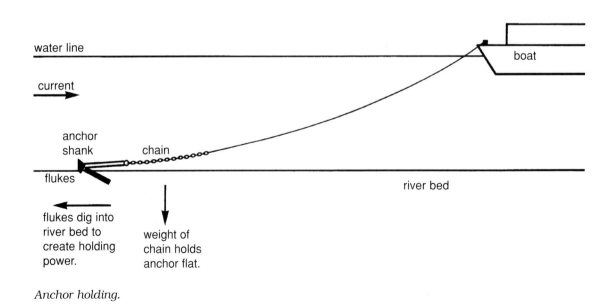

water line

current

anchor shank

chain

boat

flukes

river bed

flukes dig into river bed to create holding power.

weight of chain holds anchor flat.

Anchor holding.

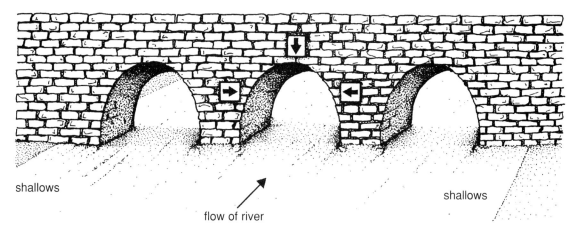

Keep to the central arch, where the water is deeper. This arch is normally indicated by arrows on the bridge itself.

at them to coincide with convenient times of the day.

Boating on the Thames or the Norfolk Broads can mean you encounter a large number of other boats as well. This will very much depend on the time of the year. This will affect the availability of moorings in certain areas – the more popular the area the less likely you are to find a suitable place to moor up immediately. You might have to go up and down the river a few times checking out the situation before you eventually find somewhere. If you don't mind moving on a bit further, and it's not too long a haul to the next moorings, then it can often save a bit of time in the long run.

You will find moorings on riverbanks miles from anywhere and with loads of room. On these occasions you might not have to pay for the privilege – but on the other hand you need to have enough food and drink on board to see you through to the morning, and possibly a pack of cards and a board game to keep you occupied. I suppose mooring fees are one of the most irritating aspects of river boating. The fact

that you have to pay in order to moor up for the night can be somewhat annoying, particularly when there are not even facilities such as a water hose or rubbish disposal from which you can benefit. It's not so bad when mooring sites do offer these services but I still sometimes think that the owners of such moorings are trying to milk the boat owner for as much as they can get.

Anchors Aweigh

All powered boats, whether narrow boats or inland cruisers, will need to have an anchor on board if you are contemplating a cruise. It is an essential part of the boat's equipment and you never know when you will need it. An anchor situated at the bow of the boat, either in an anchor locker or the bow well, is there for your safety if the power of the river starts to dominate your boat, preventing you from coping with it easily.

It may well happen that you go for many cruises without needing to use the anchor, but make sure that you are

Pontoon mooring just prior to Limehouse Lock when entering from the River Thames.

Water entering such a lock can come in with considerable force.

Lights, walkways, mooring bollards, all typical of a large lock linking a river with a canal.

The more the merrier! Plenty of diverse cruisers in this wide lock on the Caledonian Canal.

aware of its benefits nevertheless. The V-shaped type known as the Danforth, which can actually bite into the river bed and secure your boat, preventing it from being carried on unnecessarily, is the type most commonly found. Using the anchor correctly – throwing it in the water in the right place so that the boat does not ride over it – will enable you to rethink the situation and stop you drifting off with the current. An engine failure could well be one occasion for using the anchor; heading uncontrollably towards a bridge could be another.

On the Norfolk Broads and River Thames you should also have a mud anchor attached to the bow cleat of your boat. This can help in mooring up and give you additional security if there is a lot of water around you. You may tend to rotate slowly around this central point if you are stopping well away from the bank but as long as the rope is tied up firmly there is no chance of you drifting off.

Follow the basic instructions I have outlined and you should rapidly gain confidence. Experience is a great thing. Your dubious thoughts about river boating and whether you will be able to cope should soon disappear.

Points to Remember when River Cruising

1. Always take things steadily – rushing about is never going to help.
2. Before setting off keep the engine in neutral and also turn the wheel in the direction you want to go before touching the throttle.
3. Try not to go astern (use reverse) too often. You really won't be able to control the boat very easily in reverse and if you have to use it quickly and powerfully you are probably going too fast.
4. Keep your crew fully informed of what you are intending to do and also what you expect them to do.
5. Before leaving your moorings always look all around to see that the river is clear for your manoeuvrings so you don't suddenly interrupt someone else's progress.

— 12 —
Enjoying Your Boating

Of all the leisure pursuits available in this country, I believe inland waterways boating is one of the most relaxing and certainly one of the most rewarding. The other tremendous advantage it has over so many pastimes is that it is so different. How many times have you come across other folk who have said that they have always wanted to do that but never actually got round to it? It's interesting to hear some of the layman's terminology referring to 'barges' and 'long boats', but inland waterways, once you've been bitten by the bug, will become increasingly endearing as time goes on.

However you begin your first foray into canal and river cruising, it will always be an experience you'll treasure. A televized commercial may grab your attention; a series on the canal system on radio or television may encourage you to discover more and, as I mentioned earlier, sending off for brochures and catalogues will give you much more idea as to the variety of places you can visit. The hire companies vie with each other when it comes to the presentation of the boats they have available. Remember that you should always read the small print to discover exactly what is on offer, and also whether there are any hidden extras.

Your first hire holiday or your umpteenth, your first tentative cruise on the canal system of the British Isles, your maiden voyage on your newly purchased narrow boat or inland cruiser, brand new or otherwise – whatever the circum-stances, the trip will be something you'll always remember. You will want to enjoy it as best you can: short break, weekend, week, fortnight or longer. Your leisure time is precious and you will want to reap all-round benefits.

You will discover, as you travel the system, that the folk involved with inland waterways, either on a commercial or a voluntary basis, are very dedicated in what they do. The canal system was all but lost to us fifty years ago and it was only the persistence of a remarkable group of enthusiasts and the formation of the Inland Waterways Association that halted the decline. Your enjoyment of inland boating will be increased if you get involved yourself. Join the IWA, find out about your local waterways and learn about the canal society in your area. Meeting up with others and going to monthly gatherings will enable you to talk about your boating and improve it. Some folk are very well travelled and will know of places that you might not even have heard of but that are well worth visiting.

If there are any boat shows or waterways festivals on near you, go and have a look. You'll get a far wider perspective on what it's all about and discover how fascinating and diverse canals are. Buy the waterways magazines that are on sale each month. They will keep you up to date with the latest goings-on as well as containing plenty of information on boats, canal history and characters on the cut. You'll soon find that the more you

Enjoy your boating – enjoyment is what it's all about!

Part of a traditional boatman's cabin. The history of canals is a fascinating subject in itself.

know about the inland waterways system of this country, the more you will want to know.

Look in the canal and river section in your local library. You'll find a wide selection of books on the subject written by knowledgeable authors over the years. Reading up on the area you are perhaps going to be cruising shortly will be a great help and give you some idea of the local history. There are now videos being made about many canals, and put on sale. These are an excellent introduction to a waterway and will actually take you in good detail through the countryside you will be cruising. You might prefer to discover the sights for yourself, but whichever form of preparation you choose, it will certainly increase your knowledge.

Keep a record of your boating, both in the form of a log and perhaps in the form of brass plaques, which are available from canalside shops. They are attractively designed and look nice on your cabin wall. You should take pride in your boat as you travel from place to place, and should want to keep it well maintained. Have a look round chandleries. They have an enormous sclection of items on sale, some of which might be just right for your boat.

All in all, the combination of the practical handling of your boat with the discovery of more and more about our inland waterways should prove to be one of the most rewarding and satisfying pursuits that you could wish to have. Enjoy your boating safely and you will always return for another helping!

Index